The Wholehearted Woman

the wholehearted woman

Healing and Transformation in a Broken World

Laura Knutson

NASHVILLE

NEW YORK • LONDON • MELBOURNE • VANCOUVER

The Wholehearted Woman

Healing and Transformation in a Broken World

© 2023 Laura Knutson

Published in New York, New York, by Morgan James Publishing. Morgan James is a trademark of Morgan James, LLC. www.MorganJamesPublishing.com

Proudly distributed by Ingram Publisher Services.

To order additional books:
www.thewholeheartedwoman.me

Morgan James BOGO™

A **FREE** ebook edition is available for you or a friend with the purchase of this print book.

_____

CLEARLY SIGN YOUR NAME ABOVE

Instructions to claim your free ebook edition:
1. Visit MorganJamesBOGO.com
2. Sign your name CLEARLY in the space above
3. Complete the form and submit a photo of this entire page
4. You or your friend can download the ebook to your preferred device

ISBN 9781631959707 paperback
ISBN 9781631959714 ebook
Library of Congress Control Number:
2022938595

Cover Design by:
Megan Dillon
megan@creativeninjadesigns.com

Interior Design by:
Christopher Kirk
www.GFSstudio.com

Editorial:
Inspira Literary Solutions
Gig Harbor, WA

Morgan James PUBLISHING Builds with... **Habitat for Humanity** Peninsula and Greater Williamsburg

Morgan James is a proud partner of Habitat for Humanity Peninsula and Greater Williamsburg. Partners in building since 2006.

Get involved today! Visit MorganJamesPublishing.com/giving-back

To my precious granddaughters,
Abby, Izzy, Anna, and Georgia.

May your hearts be whole vessels of the love of God—
breathing it in,
soaking in it,
and giving it away.

Table of Contents

Acknowledgments

When the Lord first spoke to me about writing a book, I had no idea what a journey I was about to embark on, and I was not up to the task. I have been totally dependent on the Holy Spirit for inspiration, strength, and diligence, and all the glory is His.

Writing has been slow, and a lot of life has happened along the way. I couldn't have finished without the help of many who walked with me on this journey. I must begin with a wholehearted thank you to my faithful prayer team. Some of them have been praying for years as this manuscript has evolved; other dear friends joined along the way. These ladies have stood with me, encouraged me, and prayed for me, and I leaned heavily on their support: Jerrie, Paula, Elise, Sarah, Cathy, Jackie, Alexis, Alissa, and Jill—I treasure my friendship with each of you.

Many thanks to my editor, Arlyn Lawrence at Inspira Literary Solutions, along with her team, Kerry and Chelsea, who coached me through the process of taking a cumbersome manuscript and turning it into a readable book. You played a crucial role in bringing *The Wholehearted Woman* to publication, and your encouragement and insights were invaluable.

Thanks, also, to the team at Morgan James Publishing, for their belief in me and in the message of this book, and for their invaluable help and support in bringing it to market.

Special thanks to my husband, Mark, who has walked with me through over forty years of heart healing. My heart is still in process, and brokenness is not always easy to live with. Thank you, Mark, for your steadfastness and perseverance. I love you.

Foreword

The heart of a woman—oh, the heart of a woman; it is deep waters. Uniquely feminine, its ability to nurture and give life is unparalleled. It possesses an innate ability to relate and can navigate intense emotional situations for extended periods of time. It is powerful and fragile all at once. It can survive the Holocaust, but break down weeping over something said on the playground when it was four years old.

A woman's heart is both strong and weak. It can believe lies and deceive even the woman who owns said heart. It can lead her far away from the God who loves her and cause her to commit sins she is later deeply ashamed of.

And then there is the one whom C.S. Lewis coined "the ancient, evil genius," an Enemy whose full-time job is to study the chinks in a woman's armor and prey on her accordingly. Satan will question the truth and whisper doubts, "Did God *really* say that?. . . . . Are you *really* the daughter of God, a beloved daughter in whom He is well pleased?" He is a thief and a liar and responsible for many of our heart wounds. This is no random coincidence, as author John Eldredge points out in his book, *Wild at Heart*:

"The wound is too well aimed and far too consistent to be accidental. It was an attempt to take you out; to cripple or destroy your strength and get you out of the action. The wounds we've taken were leveled against us with stunning accuracy. . . . Do you know why there's been such an assault? The Enemy fears you. . . If you ever really got your heart back, lived from it with courage, you would be a huge problem to him. You would do a lot of damage. . . on the good side."

So, we have our own sinful nature and a lifetime of strategic wounds to contend with before we can experience wholeheartedness. Where to begin?

I must first know my place. I am not a helpless animal nor am I a goddess, decreeing right from wrong; I am a creature made by God. This means I am bound by the spiritual laws He has set in motion. It means that there is Truth, Truth I did not come up with. God has His ways; they are not my ways. They are higher.

It is in the careful study of Scripture that we find the roadmap to freedom and the motivation to obey: "I run in the path of your commands, for you have set my heart free" (Psalm 119:32). In *The Wholehearted Woman*, Laura Knutson has demonstrated how imperative it is to grasp sound doctrine in order to experience all that God has for us. No matter how you would describe your current walk with Jesus, there is always value in reviewing the bedrock of the Christian faith. "Therefore do not be foolish and thoughtless, but understand and firmly grasp what the will of the Lord is" (Ephesians 5:17).

Laura Knutson is one of the "older women" in my life and she has influenced me for the past two decades in my walk with God and as a woman, wife, and mother. It is so important that we glean from the older generation and just as important that they intentionally and earnestly pass down their hard-earned wisdom while they still can. The older generation understands which hills to die on versus what will take care of itself. Eternity feels nearer to them and they respond accordingly. In a word, they have *perspective*. We younger women would do well to listen.

While you learn from Laura, I encourage you to read the chapters one at a time and set the book down in between them. Let these truths go deep. Let them build, one thought upon another. As you work your way through, ask yourself if you have believed these words in the past. Have you seen yourself in this light? Have you seen the heart of God in your story?

Slow down to see Jesus. The gospel exposes, then embraces. Both of these can take time. Beg the Lord to show you what you don't see and what you don't want to see. Sit in any discomfort and tell Him if you don't like it; He can handle honesty. Then, watch to see how He comes to redeem your heart and make it whole again.

To Laura:
You are one of the most joyful women I have ever known. You are not afraid of the future and epitomize the Proverbs 31 woman who laughs at the days to come. Your joy is contagious and stems from your deep roots in Jesus. You have been available to me at any hour and frequently check on me like a mother would. Thank you, Laura; it is not uncommon that your one sentence of wisdom can spare me a decade of pain.

And now, dear reader, enjoy her many sentences that you presently hold in your hands.

Sarah Phillipps
Founder of She Holds Dearly
www.sheholdsdearly.com

Part One:

Join Me on a Journey

Chapter 1

My Heart's Journey

I was born a long time ago. I lived on a street full of little kids and stay-at-home moms. I had two brothers and one sister. I walked to school in the morning, walked home for lunch, then walked back to school for the afternoon. We had three recesses and occasional PE, in which we played dangerous things like circle dodge ball—in dresses. Girls did not wear pants to school.

We had a black-and-white TV with only one channel. But that didn't matter much because we were usually outside having adventures. We didn't have play dates; we just went outside and played with whomever else was out there. There was skating to be done, hide-and-seek to be played, hopscotch to be drawn on the sidewalk, and balls to be kicked and thrown around. Some lucky friends had pogo sticks or hula hoops. Inside we played board games and card games, or got out the paper and scissors and watercolors and crayons.

We went to movies occasionally, which cost thirty-five cents at the Majestic or Granada. The Majestic had a balcony, where my dad could smoke. We could get an all-day sucker that would last the whole movie for just a nickel. Popcorn was fifteen cents, but we usually couldn't shell out the money for that.

We drove clear across town to shop at the Safeway. Washoe Market was closer, but it was not as nice. Neither store was nearly as big as today's supermarkets. The cashier picked each item directly out of the basket and punched in the price by hand on the cash register. My mom paid cash. Then someone else bagged the groceries and carried them out to the car for us.

I guess you would call us something close to middle class. My dad had a company car, and my mom had a station wagon. We had food on the table, and we took some sort of vacation almost every summer. We always had clothes to wear, but not necessarily the ones we wanted. My mom sewed many of our clothes, and most of her own as well. She had a grocery budget, and she was diligent in shopping and cooking for the family. Usually, we had cereal for breakfast, sandwiches for lunch, and meat, potatoes, and a vegetable for dinner. We even ate out once or twice a year. I remember when the first McDonalds came to town, with its sign boasting an unbelievable "Over One Million Served"!

Dads went to work. Most moms, like mine, stayed home and wiped noses, cleaned bathrooms, and chauffeured kids to school and music lessons and scouts. Most of my friends lived with both their mom and their dad. If we went to a friend's house, there was usually a mom there to keep an eye on us and feed us a snack. And if we visited friends on the weekend, there was a dad around working on one project or another.

My parents worked at providing experiences for each of us, like budgeting money for my piano lessons or my older brother's ham radio equipment. They genuinely cared and provided for us. Mom was always there, and Dad came home every night. To anyone looking in from the outside, life was good. And my naïve little heart might have agreed everything was fine; I never really thought about such things.

That was my young childhood in the fifties. My formative years were typical of my era, yet specific to me. Each of us was born into circumstances that shaped our thinking and impacted our hearts. My mom grew up during the Depression and World War II. Her mom saw the transition from the horse-and-buggy to the automobile and airplane, and her life was hugely impacted by the San Francisco earthquake and the First World War. It was also my grandmother's generation who experienced Prohibition and saw women get the right to vote.

The Things that Shape Us

Politics, environment, religion, finances, family, schools, church, neighborhood, country: all these write on our hearts the answers—true or false—to our innermost questions. Add to those factors the reality of how we are treated by those closest to us, along with the implications of our own rebellious or naïve choices, and we grow up with hearts that are often hurting, confused, deceived, and broken. Even those with the finest upbringing have been affected by a fallen world. We all have hearts in need of healing.

Our outlook is shaped by what the world tells us. What we should do, how we should think, how we should look, whom we should love, what we should give, what we should take, etc. The world's systems want to answer these questions for us, but the answers keep changing. For example, there was a time when women were admired for being soft and voluptuous. Now, we should have abs of steel. There was a time when women were told their place was at home, or maybe supporting men's roles at the local school, hospital, or office. Today, a stay-at-home mom is "just" a stay-at-home mom, implying there are more influential and satisfying ways for her to make her mark.

None of the values imposed by the world have ever been able to answer our hearts' cries to know who we are. I do not see any good old days to look back to and hope for again. The world has never been a safe, wholesome place for women's hearts. Its standards are constantly fluctuating, offering us ever-mutating messages about our identities. And, with every changing standard, most of us are confronted with the uneasy feeling that we can't measure up, that we don't want to measure up, or that trying to measure up has left us deeply unsatisfied. The world feeds on wounded hearts and broken women. But the cries of a woman's heart remain:

"Who am I?"
"Am I loved?"
"What should I do?"
"Where should I go?"
"How can I give myself away and make a difference?"
"And in the midst of it all, why?"

My own childhood was actually not as "good" as it appeared on the outside. Some things were terribly wrong in my formative years. Yes, my basic physical needs were all provided. My home appeared stable. I got along well with almost everybody. I forged my way into general acceptance by teachers, classmates, and neighbors. I made good grades and was doing well at the piano. But on the inside, I was lost and insecure. I had no idea who I was or why I was here on Earth. I'm not sure exactly when it emerged, but at some point, I became aware of a deep, deep hunger for affection. I wanted to be held. To sit on a lap. To hear "I love you" from someone who nurtured my heart. My little-girl attempts at snuggling with my parents were rebuffed in both action and word, and I eventually gave up. On the outside, I seemed normal and fine. On the inside, my heart was wounded, unfulfilled, and shriveling up.

I think my parents did the best they could with what they had. Their hearts were wounded too, and they didn't have real affection to give. I never told my mom about my hunger for affection, but in her later years, she shared with me that there had been none in her own childhood. A popular parenting expert had informed her parents' generation that too much cuddling would spoil a child. And a doctor told my mom that my brother, her firstborn, should be potty trained before he was one year old! Not only did she not have any childhood experience of what warmth and nurturing felt like, but she was encouraged to stifle her own natural desire to hold her children close. Add to that the extreme pressure to perform ("get him potty trained before he's a year old"), with the resulting guilt of not being up to the task, and you have one hopeless and frustrated mother. And this just scratches the surface of her pain.

Challenges like these barely open a window to the tragic experiences that have shattered the hearts and destroyed the identities of so many women! As you are reading this, I'm sure experiences from your own childhood are surfacing. Maybe you are remembering things you haven't thought of for decades. Perhaps certain experiences nag at your heart and mind—things you can never forget, things that color your whole perspective of the world. Perhaps you can never remember being happy, loved, or carefree.

None of us is unscathed. Each of us who has lived in this fallen world has been affected to some degree by brokenness. Disappointments, betrayal, neglect, abandonment, rejection, withholding, abuses, illness, loss . . . these can leave our hearts angry, hardened, deceived, jealous, grieving, vengeful, fearful, and hopeless. And our sense of identity and purpose is filtered through that brokenness.

The Journey to Wholeness

Injustices against women are front-page news, as is the movement to right these wrongs and promote our welfare. The world today broadcasts our plight and has dictated a solution: rise up (in an almost militant fashion) and forge our own way into significance and power. If we could only oversee our own destiny and do away with anything that opposes us, then we could be whole and happy. But being in charge won't heal our hearts. Being the leader won't ultimately tell us who we are or where we should go. We may coerce the world into putting us in positions we think will make us happy, but in the end, our hearts will still be hurting, deceived, and unfulfilled.

The enemy of our souls—the devil—loves it when our hearts break. He slithers through the damaged chambers and uses our pain to lie to us about who we are. He has targeted our hearts and challenged our identities from the beginning of time. Sometimes, we have bought into his lies. Sometimes, we have fought one lie with another. We may even give up our dreams and passions because he convinces us there's just too much opposition.

God's design is for our hearts to be whole, unbroken, unhindered vessels of His love. We were designed to receive it, ingest it, and give it away. The greater our capacity to receive God's love, the greater our influence for good. And make no mistake: we were created to have a *powerful* influence.

Our identities as women flow from the image and heart of God. Our identities must come from who *He* says we are. As we connect to God in intimacy and to His Word in wisdom, our hearts begin to heal and we become who we were created to be. Transformed lives emerge as we hear our Father speak the truth about us and as our hearts are touched by His love.

The journey to wholeness is not quick or easy. Many of us have spent our lives trying to forge our identities with our choices and actions. We expend huge amounts of energy proving to ourselves and others who we are and what we can do. Many of us entertain an awful lot of guilt and regret: "If only I had done *that*, I would be a worthy woman and my life would be better." We carry anger and bitterness: "If only they hadn't done *that* to me, I could be whole." We carry unbelief: "If God really loved me, I wouldn't be dealing with *this*." Some of us carry huge amounts of emotional pain which cripples our ability to think or act on any level.

Whole hearts and transformed lives flow from understanding our real identities. It's a lifelong journey that will both satisfy us and make us hungry for more. It will thrill us; it will overwhelm us. And it will impact this world and all of eternity. I invite you on that journey.

Chapter 1 Reflection

1. How has your heart been reacting as you read my story?

_____

_____

_____

_____

2. What parts of your own story have been brought to mind?

_____

_____

_____

_____

3. Is your heart hungry for this journey? Indifferent? Curious? Fearful?

_____

_____

_____

_____

_____

_____

Chapter 2

This Heart of Mine

Ah, the heart. It has been written about, sung about, fought over, celebrated, and mourned since time immemorial. Consider these quotes from a variety of centuries and continents:

Wherever you go, go with all your heart.
—Confucius (Chinese, 551–479 BC)

Every heart sings a song . . .
—Plato (Greek, approximately 428–348 BC)

Thou hast made us for thyself, O Lord,
and our heart is restless until it finds its rest in thee.
—Augustine of Hippo (Roman Berber, AD 354–430)

Grant that I may not pray alone with the mouth;
help me that I may pray from the depths of my heart.
—Martin Luther (German, AD 1483–1546)

The heart has its reasons which reason knows not.
—Blaise Pascal (French, AD 1623–1662)

I put my heart and my soul into my work,
and I have lost my mind in the process.
—Vincent Van Gogh (Dutch, AD 1853–1890)

The most beautiful things in the world cannot be seen
or even touched; they must be felt with the heart.
—Helen Keller (American, AD 1880–1968)

What is this heart they are all talking about? None of these quotes is about the organ that pumps blood through the body—nor is this book. "Heart" is one of those words we use to mean many things, so a working definition is important to nail down.

Dictionary.com defines the heart as "the center of the total personality, especially with reference to intuition, feeling, or emotion." Merriam-Webster says it can refer to "one's innermost character, feelings, or inclinations." The word most often translated "heart" in the Old Testament can signify feelings, will, intellect, the inner man, soul, and conscience. Strong's Concordance suggests the word most often translated "heart" in the New Testament can be defined as "the fountain and seat of the thoughts, passions, desires, appetites, affections, purposes, endeavors." Proverbs 4:23 states it succinctly for us: "Above all else, guard your heart, *for everything you do flows from it*." For the purposes of this book, we will define "heart" as the *inner fountain of passion, thought, and purpose.*

The word "whole" also has different meanings. It can mean complete, undivided, the entirety of something. But it also means healthy, perfect, undiminished, not injured in any way, and lacking nothing. Both meanings can apply to our hearts.

God did not give any of us just a portion of a heart. We each have an *inner fountain of passion, thought, and purpose* from which everything flows, and it's not lacking any of its parts. But it is also not perfectly healthy or undamaged. My whole heart has been affected by life, and it is not whole.

The Whole Heart of God

Having a heart is part of what it means to be created in God's image. Our judgments about our identities and our lives flow from our hearts. Our hearts tell us who we are, how we should act, and what we should pursue. That's how we were designed! We were made in the image of God, and He certainly acts from His heart: "I will rejoice in doing them good and will assuredly plant them in this land with all my heart and soul" (Jeremiah 32:41).

God's heart is whole: there is no conflict between what is true, how He feels, and how He acts. His heart is informed by nothing but truth. But if our own hearts are informed by lies and the effects of betrayal, abandonment, rejection, abuse, and all the various evils that have influenced us, then our thinking, acting, feeling, and pursuing will be misled. We will be blind to the glorious truth about our identities and purposes. The results will be disastrous. The results *have been* disastrous. To the degree our lives flow from damaged, deceived hearts, we bring destruction upon ourselves and the world around us.

The heart is referred to over nine hundred times in the Bible. God created us with hearts, knows each of our hearts intimately, and wants our hearts to be whole. He understands the joys and the perils of having the hearts He has given us.

I spent some time with the concordance one afternoon discovering the ways our hearts are described in the Bible. This is not even a complete list:

- Unbelieving heart
- Hard heart
- Deceived heart
- Doubting heart
- Pure heart
- Discouraged heart
- Obstinate heart
- Stout heart
- Trusting heart
- Proud heart
- Faint heart
- Wise heart
- Sad heart
- Evil heart
- Afflicted heart
- Generous heart
- Cheerful heart
- Boastful heart
- Troubled heart
- Secret heart
- Merry heart
- Contrite heart
- Straying heart
- Blameless heart
- Faithful heart
- Perverse heart
- Unfeeling heart
- Willing heart
- Anxious heart
- Sick heart
- Bitter heart
- Obedient heart
- Rejoicing heart
- Aching heart
- Raging heart
- Envious heart
- Unsearchable heart
- Calloused heart
- Tender heart
- Heavy heart
- Righteous heart
- Striving heart
- Hasty heart
- True heart
- Angry heart
- Glad heart
- Dull heart
- Feeble heart
- Courageous heart
- Vengeful heart

- Lying heart
- Clean heart
- Rebellious heart
- Wounded heart
- Tranquil heart
- Burning heart
- False heart
- Yearning heart
- Captivated heart
- Broken heart
- Overflowing heart
- Impenitent heart
- Sincere heart
- Grieved heart

Did you find your heart in some of those descriptions? I would love to have a heart that reflects some of those terms. Others, I could live without, thank you very much!

We are commanded to love the Lord with whole hearts, serve Him with whole hearts, seek Him with whole hearts, and trust Him with whole hearts. We are encouraged to do all things wholeheartedly. But if our hearts aren't whole to begin with, that is a problem. I have learned from experience that applying the entirety of my wounded, deceived heart to the things before me will not bring the fulfilling life I desire. What, then, can we do with these hearts? Where do we find healing? How can we address the crippling effects of lies and circumstances and see our hearts become whole? How can we become wholehearted women?

Fellow traveler, the Lord knows our hearts. He knows they are central to our lives. That's why He asks us to care for them—because He knows their importance, and He knows the dangers they are susceptible to. That's why our Proverbs verse says (in another version): "Watch over your heart with all diligence, for from it flow the springs of life" (Proverbs 4:23, NASB).

In His grace, the Lord never asks us to do something He does not empower us to do. None of us has the wisdom to care for our hearts on our own. We don't know all the dangers or how to avoid them. But He has empowered us by giving us tools. We have the Father Himself, after whose heart ours were fashioned. We have the Holy Spirit, who is our Teacher, Counselor, and Companion along the way. We have Jesus, who is our Healer, Savior, and Redeemer. We have the Bible, the owner's manual for the human heart. Our hearts *can* be taught and comforted, healed and made whole.

The glory of womanhood has not changed with time. There are truths for us to embrace and live by regardless of our time or circumstances. Each of us has a different story, but the path to healing involves the same wisdom and truth for all. There is no system, no experience, no healing that the world can offer to bring us into wholeness. All the answers are in the hands of the One who created our hearts in the first place. He is not shocked by our feelings or threatened by our questions. He says He loves us and He will never leave us or forsake us. He says we are not alone, and He wants to have a relationship with us. He says He can take our painful pasts and use them for our good.

Can all this be true? Can we really come to an understanding of who we are and why we are here? Can we really know God? Does He really know us? Can the unspoken desires of our hearts be met? Can the broken places be filled with peace and joy? Can we move forward with whole hearts?

My friend, I believe the answer is yes. It is happening for me, and I've seen it happening in many others, some of whom started their journey with much more brokenness than I. Each of us has an identity that flows from the heart of God. By His grace and power, we can wrestle our identities back from our pasts and live with whole hearts.

Chapter 2 Reflection

1. How often are you aware of your own passions, thoughts, and purposes?

_____

_____

_____

_____

_____

2. Which ones of the heart descriptions connect with you? How or why?

_____

_____

_____

_____

_____

3. Is there another adjective that you would use to describe your heart?

_____

_____

_____

_____

_____

Chapter 3

Bring Your Whole Heart

J esus said something strange in His Sermon on the Mount: "Blessed
are those who mourn, for they will be comforted" (Matthew 5:4).
This is one of the sayings of Jesus known as the Beatitudes. Most
of us are familiar with these verses in Matthew 5:3–12 which describe
circumstances and heart conditions Jesus calls blessed.

As I meditated on this particular Beatitude, it looked like a great
contradiction to me. I could see the spiritual value in other qualities
mentioned in the Beatitudes. Meekness, hunger for righteousness, mercy,
purity, peacemaking: I could comprehend the blessedness in all of that.
But grieving, loss, mourning? *That* would make me blessed?

Mourning is an emotional response to loss. And, as we've established,
the heart of each one of us has been affected by loss. That loss comes in so
many guises! Wrecked relationships, broken promises, loss of children or
spouses, ruined reputations, failed ministries, personal failures, physical
hardships, destroyed dreams. We have lost much, and our hearts have
been wounded. How can God call us blessed when our hearts want to
shrivel up and die?

What are some of the ways we handle our pain? Stuff it down, drown it out with busyness, ignore it, medicate it? We may throw ourselves a little pity party, and then expect to get over the pain and get on with life. A supposedly "Christian" response might be a stiff upper lip: "God is good, and I am fine. I can do this. If I just speak enough truth to myself and claim enough promises, this will pass." Some of those strategies may bring us temporary relief and enable us to keep going, but they rob us of something important.

For some of us, the pain causes us to turn our backs on our feelings altogether and shut down our hearts. We keep doing the things we should, but our hearts are not in it because we have denied them their influence in our lives. It seems easier to live without feeling at all than to live with the pain. For others, the pain is so great, it takes them out of the game. Fear, shame, or depression keep them from seeing any way forward. What can we do? God calls us blessed, right in the middle of our pain. But how? Why?

The answer lies in the promise from the second half of our verse: ". . . for they shall be comforted." Fascinating. If we look at the second halves of other Beatitudes, we find some amazing promises. Ours is the Kingdom of Heaven (we get that promise twice)! We inherit the earth! We are filled with righteousness, we are shown mercy, we see God, and He calls us His kids! Those are awesome promises, and at first glance, they seem to be in a class above mere "comfort."

The Apostle Paul calls our Father the God of all comfort. And he says comfort should be a part of our life together. We are to receive it from God, and we are to give it away:

> *Praise be to the God and Father of our Lord Jesus Christ, the*
> *Father of compassion and the God of all comfort, who comforts*
> *us in all our troubles, so that we can comfort those in any*
> *trouble with the comfort we ourselves receive from God.*
>
> *(2 Corinthians 1:3–4)*

Receiving God's Comfort

What is it about comfort that makes it so valuable?

I think we need to start by letting God show us a whole new vision of what comfort is. We *could* say, "Well, thanks, God. You let me go through this horrific time, and then You take me in your arms and tell me you understand because You've suffered too. You pat me on the back, say 'There, there,' and tell me I'm blessed. I just don't really feel blessed in all this." But let's dig deeper and really hear the promise. God says there is a blessing in my pain. That blessing is comfort. And comfort is ranked right up there with important things like righteousness and the Kingdom of Heaven. Is our picture of God's comfort way too small?

Comfort does not target our enemies, or our problems, or our foolishness. It is not a hand reaching out to pull us from our misery. It is not a clinical procedure to clean out the muck and promote healing. It is not a set of directions for walking in wholeness. Comfort acknowledges the pain without trying to fix it or reason it away.

Comfort does not speak to our actions or our motives. It does not call us to change our minds about something or to forgive someone. It does not suggest a necessary modification of attitudes or behaviors. It requires absolutely nothing of us except to mourn. Comfort targets the pain in our hearts.

Ladies, let this speak to you about how important your heart is. The Creator of the universe knows your pain and wants to meet you right in the middle of it. Full stop. No ifs, ands, or buts. The comfort He offers is simply His own knowing, loving presence. He *knows*, He *sees*, and He *is there*. You are not alone. Your heart is not hopelessly lost, floating somewhere at sea where no one can find or rescue it. Your heart is known and felt by the One who created it in the first place.

And this Comforter is One who gets it. Jesus took on flesh just like ours. He felt the effects of abuse, misunderstanding, false accusation, and rejection. And He felt something we will never have to feel: God abandoned Him! The Father had to turn His face from Jesus when our sins were placed on His shoulders at the cross. Jesus totally surrendered Himself to the sufferings of the world: "He was despised and rejected by men, a man of sorrows and acquainted with grief. . ... Surely he has borne our griefs and carried our sorrows" (Isaiah 53:3-4, ESV).

There are many facets of regaining wholeness for our hearts, but I believe the first step is just to acknowledge the brokenness. Do you carry sorrow? Grief? You don't even have to be able to identify or articulate the pain. You may recognize that you are unhappy, or dull, or angry, or confused, without knowing why. God knows. He *knows*. He is intimately acquainted with your grief. And you don't have to tell Him what's wrong or improve in some way before you invite Him in. The first step to wholeheartedness is vulnerability and helplessness. "Here I am, God," you may pray. "I don't know what to do. I don't even know exactly what's wrong." The promise of comfort makes this kind of vulnerability possible.

By the time my parents divorced during the year I turned fifteen, I had completely shut down my heart. I had no emotional response to anything. Given the choice of which parent to live with, I chose my dad. Actually, I chose his new wife. In retrospect, although I was not aware of it at the time, I see my heart was holding out some hope for the motherly affection my own mom had not been able to give me. I didn't get it there either, but my heart was so numb by then it really didn't matter much.

I occupied myself by simply doing what was in front of me. I had no confidence, no sense of joy or adventure. I only committed to things I thought I could do well. I had no vision for my life because vision requires some sort of passion. But I was actually quite proud of how I was handling life. I observed other girls living in their drama: some cried, some made foolish choices, some entered stupid relationships, some agonized over practically everything. I thought myself above all that, and it made my life so much simpler!

I would not—could not—have acknowledged that my heart was broken. But God knew! He had to circumvent my proud thoughts and dead heart to begin to get through to me. And He did it as only He could, in His wisdom, and love, and creativity.

Beginning the Healing Journey

I graduated from college with a degree in music. At the time, I was working enough as a musician and piano teacher to pay my half of the expenses, living in a little rental cottage with a roommate. I had no plans, hopes, or ambitions for marriage, a career, anything. I was just doing the next thing. I knew nothing of God, but had gotten curious about Him because I met some other music people who talked about Him (and Jesus) as if they knew Him.

I bought myself one of the books I noticed them reading: Ralph Martin's *Hungry for God*. (I would have told you I wasn't hungry. Just curious.) But as I sat alone reading one afternoon, the words faded and I saw a vision of a man, standing far off in a field of tall grass. His arms were open wide to me, and He simply said, "Come."

I fell apart. Completely. I curled up on my little sofa and cried from the depths of my soul. Through my tears I wailed, "I'm coming."

I could not have told you at the time it was Jesus who had appeared to me. I had no understanding of the simplest doctrines of Christianity. I didn't know I was a sinner in need of a savior. I didn't understand who Jesus was, or why He had died. I did not repent. The only profession I made was that I was coming. I didn't know whom I had just promised to follow or where He might take me. But He had connected to my heart in an instant, and there was something about His presence that won me. My desperate, thirsty heart saw a stream of water, and it ran for a drink.

Decades later, I came to understand what God had really done in that moment. He knew that inside me was a little girl who just wanted to be welcomed into loving arms. He was inviting me into an embrace! God had targeted my heart, touching it with the kind of comfort it needed, the kind it had been starved of for so long. And this little girl was able to respond! Comfort blossomed into hope, and hunger, and pursuit. This was the beginning of my journey.

I share this story only as an example. God will not touch us all in the same way, because we all need something different. But rest assured: your heart has a great big bull's eye on it, and God is focused on the center. He doesn't shoot arrows of information or instruction at you. He brings Himself, His love, His comfort. Of course, we eventually need information and instruction as well! We need to engage our minds and our wills in our journey to wholeness. Comfort is only a piece of the journey, but it is a crucial piece. It may not be the beginning point for you, but it will come where and when His wisdom moves. I talk about comfort first to encourage you to bring your needy heart to Jesus. Whatever your path to salvation and wholeness, you will meet comfort along the way.

I cannot tell you what comfort might look like or feel like for you. God knows your pain more intimately than even you do, and He knows best how to reach you. Perhaps you will sense the tiniest bit of light on the horizon, just enough to encourage you to get up and hope once more. Maybe you will feel a tinge of joy you can see no reason for. Or maybe it will just be some peace, a bit of breathing space where you didn't expect it. Paul writes in Philippians 4:7 about "the peace that transcends understanding," a peace that has no rational reason to exist. You may even feel guilty for daring to feel some peace in the midst of life's chaos! That peace is a visitation of comfort from your Father. Embrace it as a gift, and let it draw you to Him.

Wholeheartedness is a lifelong journey. God has revealed Himself to us in His story, the Bible. He calls us to learn, grow, and change. Like everyone who embarks on this journey, I had to learn the story. I had to repent and receive His forgiveness. I am still being transformed; I am so far from perfect! But my heart has found its resting place. His comfort is my oasis in the desert, my steady place in the storm. It's not only a place where I learn; it's a place where my broken heart receives a healing touch.

The prophet Isaiah spoke of the comfort Jesus would bring to His people:

> *The Spirit of the Sovereign* LORD *is on me, because the* LORD *has anointed me to proclaim good news to the poor. He has sent me to bind up the brokenhearted . . .to comfort all who mourn, and provide for those who grieve in Zion—to bestow on them a crown of beauty instead of ashes, the oil of joy instead of mourning, and a garment of praise instead of a spirit of despair.*
> *(Isaiah 61:1–3)*

Bring your mourning and your grief! Don't try to leave them behind. There is a trade-off in the visitation of God's comfort: He promises the blessings of beauty, joy, and praise in exchange for ashes, mourning, and despair. You may not feel it right away. Your loving Father may start your journey in a different place. But your heart is known and precious to Jesus, and it is safe on this journey. Wherever He meets you, and wherever He takes you, dare to bring your whole broken heart.

Chapter 3 Reflection

1. I described many kinds of losses in this chapter. Are there personal losses that came to mind while you were reading?

_____

_____

_____

2. Describe some of the ways that you have dealt with loss in the past.

_____

_____

_____

_____

3. Have you had personal experiences of God's comfort? Describe them.

_____

_____

_____

4. How would you have described comfort before reading this chapter? Do you have a different perspective now? Are you finding yourself encouraged to "bring your whole heart"?

_____

_____

_____

Part Two:
Our Hearts' Origin Story

Created Hearts

Satan watched in wonder as God took a handful of dust and fashioned a new creature. This new being was different from all the others. Unlike the other creatures—including himself—Satan could see this creature had the imprint of God on him. The glory of God that Satan had witnessed in heaven shone from this creature. Hmmm. . .

Satan's eyes were now glued to the events unfolding on Earth. He watched in dismay as God stooped down and breathed His own breath into this creature, which he called Adam. The Enemy was beginning to feel uneasy. Adam had something Satan couldn't quite identify, and he was disturbed by it. The breath of God had brought—how could he describe it?—a thinking, feeling, caring, creative capacity. It threatened him. Well, at least there was just one of these creatures.

Then God put Adam to sleep. Even better.

But wait—what was this? God was reaching into the man and pulling out part of him. God was fashioning that part into a second *creature! This new one glowed with that same glory. It was like the first one, yet drastically different. There was that thinking and feeling and caring and creating, but it felt different, came from a different perspective. And now that same breath and image were carried by two creatures.*

Satan felt equally threatened by both. The world was beginning to feel like an unsafe place.

Oh, horror of horrors, God wasn't finished yet. He just gave these creatures authority over this whole earth! He made them His partners and shared His authority with them. Fear and rage filled Satan. He wanted all the glory and the power for himself!

The nightmare continued. Satan realized it would not just be those two. God was instructing them to have offspring— lots of them—and fill the whole earth! How many would there be, these image bearers and co-rulers with God?

To pursue whole hearts, we must have a basic understanding of the origin and nature of ourselves and our hearts. How did we get here? And why?

Characters do not make up their own origin stories; their stories originate with the writer. And we have a Writer and Creator who has revealed our origin story. The Author of Life does not intend for us to guess at answers to our heart's questions. He has provided us with an outline of the whole narrative, complete with historical details, future plans, and our roles and purposes along the way. Let's take a look.

We will approach the subject of our hearts from an unapologetically biblical worldview. Our *inner fountains of passion, thought, and purpose* are unique among all living things. The human heart is not the result of random collisions of time, energy, and matter. The capacity to entertain passions, thoughts, and purposes did not evolve from other life forms. These hearts, and we who carry them, originated in the heart of God and were created in His image. The nature and purpose of our hearts were established at the foundation of the world.

Why You Were Created

In Genesis, we learn God created a world out of nothing. He introduced everything in order: light; sky, sea, and land; vegetation; sun, moon, and stars; sea creatures, birds, and land animals. He was deliberate about each detail, preparing a place for the crown of creation, mankind:

> *And the LORD God formed man of the dust of the ground, and breathed into his nostrils the breath of life; and man became a living soul.*
>
> *(Genesis 2:7, KJV)*

> *God said, "Let Us make mankind in Our image, according to Our likeness; and let them rule over the fish of the sea and over the birds of the sky and over the livestock and over all the earth, and over every crawling thing that crawls on the earth."*
>
> *(Genesis 1:26, NASB 2020)*

The entirety of mankind, male and female, was represented in Adam:

> *So God created mankind in His image; in the image of God He created him; male and female He created them.*
>
> *(Genesis 1:27, NASB 2020)*

Mankind is the pinnacle of creation, distinct from the rest of creation. We are the only creatures made in the image of God. We receive our life from the very breath of God.

God created the earth for mankind. And in mankind, He created for Himself a partner and friend. Unlike the other creatures, Adam and Eve each had a heart, an *inner fountain of passion, thought, and purpose.* They were not directed by mere instinct. They had spiritual and creative passions. They could relate to God, know Him, and love Him. They shared in the purposes and desires of God. They were entrusted with authority; they could embody the wisdom of God in exercising dominion over creation. They could think, create, plan, and build. Their motivation was not limited to survival or fun. Their hearts could grasp eternal purposes.

And what are these eternal purposes? The Bible gives us some clear answers:

- To bear the image of God on the earth: "Then God said, 'Let us make mankind in our image, in our likeness'." (Genesis 1:26)
- To increase in number, filling the earth with that image: "Be fruitful and increase in number; multiply on the earth and increase upon it." (Genesis 1:28)
- To reflect the glory of God, taking that glory with us and filling the earth with it as we multiply. He says we are children "called by my name, whom I created for my glory, whom I formed and made. . . . the people I formed for myself that they may proclaim my praise." (Isaiah 43:7,21) Throughout Scripture, angels proclaim this truth: "Holy, holy, holy is the LORD Almighty; the whole earth is full of his glory." (Isaiah 6:3)
- To reflect the character of God by caring for His creation. He has given mankind the role of stewardship "so that they may rule over the fish in the sea and the birds in the sky, over the livestock and all the wild animals, and over all the creatures that move along the ground." (Genesis 1:26).

- To reflect the love of God by caring for each other: "Love one another. As I have loved you, so you must love one another." (John 13:34-35)

God is on display in all His glory in heaven, and angels look on Him in wonder. And as the angels gaze at the earth, they look also on mankind in wonder. I can imagine them marveling, "Look! They are not like us, and they are not the same as the rest of creation! We see the very imprint of God on them!" God's design and care for humans are beyond what even they can grasp: "Even angels long to look into these things." (1 Peter 1:12)

Let's put the pieces together. God made Adam and Eve in His own image. Imbued with that image, with the very heart of God, they were to rule over creation. Adam and Eve, whom God established in the Garden of Eden, were given the mandate to multiply and fill the whole earth. And why? So the whole earth would be filled with God's glory!

God has plans for you and your heart! They are good plans! And don't miss this: God has not dropped mankind off on the earth to let us figure things out on our own. He intends for us to walk in relationship with Him, experiencing His love:

I have loved you with an everlasting love; I have drawn you with unfailing kindness.

(Jeremiah 31:3)

Give thanks to the LORD, for he is good. His love endures forever.
(Psalm 136:1)

He wants us to seek Him and His wisdom as we carry out His purposes. And He is a generous friend and provider:

Ask and it will be given to you; seek and you will find; knock and the door will be opened to you.

(Matthew 7:7)

If any of you lacks wisdom, you should ask God, who gives generously to all without finding fault, and it will be given to you.

(James 1:5)

All His plans for us are good, and they will prevail:

"For I know the plans I have for you," declares the LORD, "plans to prosper you and not to harm you, plans to give you hope and a future."

(Jeremiah 29:11)

The plans of the LORD stand firm forever, the purposes of his heart through all generations.

(Psalm 33:11)

The human heart—*your* heart—was incubated in the heart of God and formed with eternal wisdom and love. There is nothing random or accidental about your existence. You are here *on purpose*. You are the only one like you *on purpose*. You have a heart *on purpose*. You carry unique thoughts, talents, hopes, and characteristics *on purpose*. That heart of yours is like no other, and its value is immeasurable. God started with two people, but His plan was to fill the earth with image-bearing friends. You are one of them. Let no one devalue your heart by creating for it a false origin story.

And God saw all that He had made, and behold, it was very good.
(Genesis 1:31, NASB 2020)

Chapter 4 Reflection

1. What are the ways that mankind is different from the rest of the creation?

_____

_____

_____

_____

2. What is the origin story you have believed about yourself? How does the biblical narrative impact your passions, thoughts, and purposes?

_____

_____

_____

_____

3. Why does Satan hate all of us?

_____

_____

_____

_____

_____

_____

Chapter 5

Broken Hearts

Satan's eyes narrowed.

"These two must be destroyed at all costs. They must not know who they are, who God is, or who I am! Their passions and thoughts must be confused and twisted. They must not be allowed to grasp a vision of their purpose. I cannot let them trust this God.

"But how to do it? How to break this partnership with God? How to separate them from each other? How to trick them into following me instead of God?

"Can it be done? If I twist God's words a little, and offer them something with immediate appeal, will they fall for it? God has given them authority over the whole world. Can I get them to hand that authority to me?

"If I don't try, they will destroy me. If I succeed, God's plans will be thwarted, their hearts will be darkened, and I will rule!"

T
here they were. Adam and Eve were perfect co-laborers, perfectly designed by God, set in Eden's perfect environment. They had unbroken fellowship with God and with each other. But things are not perfect in our present day. Not at all. What has happened? And what can be done about it?

We last left the man and woman in the Garden of Eden, where God had placed them to begin to rule the world and fill it with the His glory. In His presence, they had absolute dominion and freedom. Except for one Do Not Touch sign:

> *The LORD God took the man and put him in the Garden of Eden to work it and take care of it. And the LORD God commanded the man, "You are free to eat from any tree in the garden; but you must not eat from the tree of the knowledge of good and evil, for when you eat from it you will certainly die.*
>
> *(Genesis 2:15-17)*

The story continues in the third chapter of Genesis:

> *Now the serpent was more crafty than any of the wild animals the LORD God had made. He said to the woman, "Did God really say, 'You must not eat from any tree in the garden'?" The woman said to the serpent, "We may eat fruit from the trees in the garden, but God did say, 'You must not eat fruit from the tree that is in the middle of the garden, and you must not touch it, or you will die.'"*
>
> *"You will not certainly die," the serpent said to the woman. "For God knows that when you eat from it your eyes will be opened, and you will be like God, knowing good and evil."*
>
> *(Genesis 3:1–5)*

This tree is often spoken of as an apple tree, but notice that the exact identity of the fruit of this tree is unknown. It is not crucial to the story. The critical thing about this fruit was that God had said not to eat it!

The issue here is not what we do or do not eat. The issue is lordship. Adam and Eve were given *carte blanche* to enjoy what God had created for them, with one exception. God's desire was for Adam and Eve to remain in relationship with Him and honor Him with obedient hearts. God did not demand obedience to a huge list of rules, but rather a single command intended to let them choose to trust His leadership.

A Crucial Question

This is the core question we must ask ourselves: *Who has the wisdom and responsibility to discern what is right or wrong for us?* If we give God that place in our lives, then we will trust His judgments about what is good and evil.

Eve chose to circumvent God (and elevate herself) by determining right and wrong apart from Him:

> And when the woman saw that the tree was good for food, and that it was delightful to look at, and a tree to be desired in order to make one wise and insightful, she took some of its fruit and ate it; and she also gave some to her husband with her, and he ate.
> (Genesis 3:6, AMP)

Eve betrayed her own heart, which had been fashioned to love and honor God! In choosing to follow Satan, she rejected her relationship with God. Hers was the first sin, and hers was the first broken heart.

No, Adam and Eve did not drop dead the minute they ate of the tree. God had not been warning them about physical death. Their death was a spiritual one: in rejecting their relationship to God as Creator, Lord, and Father, they alienated their hearts from the One who gave them life. They introduced sin—rebellion against God's lordship—into the world.

This one act affected all of us who have come after them. Remember: Adam and Eve had been given dominion over all of creation. When they disobeyed God, they thought they were choosing self-rule. But they were actually submitting themselves to Satan and bringing the rest of creation down with them. Because of Adam and Eve, our hearts and the world were under Satan's dominion before we were born. All of us, descended from their seed, were born into a world that is in bondage to sin and separated from God.

How has this separation impacted our hearts?

First, it broke our fellowship with the heart of God: "Your iniquities have separated you from your God; your sins have hidden his face from you, so that he will not hear." (Isaiah 59:2)

How can my heart bear that? God has hidden His face from me, and He won't even listen to me! This heart, created for fellowship with my God, was born into a world separated from Him. My heart was born hungry into a world in which nothing could satisfy it.

Second, the hearts of mankind, which were created to experience and spread the goodness and righteousness of God, have become slaves to Satan and are in bondage to sin:

> *"Don't you know that when you offer yourselves [like Adam and Eve] to someone [in this case, Satan] as obedient slaves, you are slaves of the one you obey—whether you are slaves to sin, which leads to death, or to obedience, which leads to righteousness [right relationship with God]?"*
>
> *(Romans 6:16)*

Not only is my heart now under the dominion of Satan, but the power of sin persuades my heart to think, act, and feel in ways that only bring more woundedness. And sin's power is drawing those around me to make choices that will wound their own hearts *and* mine! I am both perpetrator and victim, at the mercy of the malevolent power to which Adam and Eve surrendered the world.

Underlying all of this, we have a serious legal problem. Our glorious God is not only perfect in love, perfect in grace, and perfect in wisdom. He is also *just*. His nature requires that evil and rebellion be punished. A god who would allow wickedness and rebellion to flourish unopposed could not ultimately be good. And the God who created the earth to be filled with His glory could not simply turn a blind eye to the corrupting and putrefying spread of evil.

Adam and Eve, who had once lived under the favor of God, placed themselves in opposition to Him. Therefore, His justice demanded a death sentence, for "the wages of sin is death." (Romans 6:23)

God says in Isaiah 13:11, "I will punish the world for its evil, the wicked for their sins. I will put an end to the arrogance of the haughty and will humble the pride of the ruthless." This is a catastrophic blow to our hearts! Unless we are rescued, our hearts will never be whole. To begin with, our fellowship with our Father must be restored so we can again bask in His love and hear His voice. His love must work deeply in our hearts, restoring the broken places. And the oppressive cloud of judgment must be lifted from us. A heart cannot thrive under the threat of doom.

The power which sin wields in our hearts must also be broken. My *inner fountain of passion, thought, and purpose* is subject to a power that moves it toward actions and decisions that bring devastation. The power of sin is too great for me to overcome on my own. I can grit my teeth and exercise an iron will to do what is right, but I am ultimately no match for the power of evil at loose in this fallen world. I will win some skirmishes—perhaps many of them—but I will eventually wear out and give in before the war is over. Paul recognized this predicament in himself:

> *I have the desire to do what is good, but I cannot carry it out.* . . . .
> *For in my inner being I delight in God's law; but I see another law*
> *at work in me, waging war against the law of my mind and making*
> *me a prisoner of the law of sin at work within me.*
> *(Romans 7:18,22–23)*

The good news is that the gospel of Jesus Christ has the solution for all these problems! We *can* be restored to unbroken fellowship with our God. We *can* get out from under that cloud of judgment. We *can* be snatched back from the Enemy. Sin's power in us *can* be broken!

Wouldn't you love to see all that happen in an instant? *Poof!* We would walk in the garden again in unbroken fellowship with God. *Shazam!* Our hearts would stop making stupid choices, and we wouldn't keep wounding ourselves and others. *Voila!* The sun would always shine, everything would always work, and peace would never end.

Well, ladies, that's how the world was designed in Eden. But God deliberately included an option that He knew could bring it all down. And He did it for the sake of our hearts.

If our hearts are ever to experience the fullness of love, there must be a choice on our part. Love has no meaning outside of choosing. If I am a skin-and-bones apparatus without the ability to ignore, disdain, or injure someone, then my love for others is meaningless and their love for me is hollow. If my heart is merely a hardwired machine, then thinking, feeling, and acting are robotic. My *inner fountain of passion, thought, and purpose* is just a computer chip.

The root of it all is *relationship*, which is based in choice. And if this goodness is something we are empowered to choose, then evil must be an option as well. God allowed evil, personified in Satan, to present itself. And Adam and Eve fell for it. The world, and our hearts, fell with them.

Paul felt the devastating impact of this reality: "What an agonizing situation I am in! So who has the power to rescue this miserable man from the unwelcome intruder of sin and death?" (Romans 7:24, TPT)

Our hearts echo Paul's cry: *Who will rescue us?*

Chapter 5 Reflection

1. Have you wrestled with the question of who has the best plan for your life? What are the ways and reasons you have opposed God's leadership?

_____

_____

_____

_____

_____

2. Have you been consciously aware of the existence of evil? Have you seen any purpose in it, or have you resented it?

_____

_____

_____

_____

3. How would you define sin?

_____

_____

_____

_____

4. Is there sometimes a conflict between the things you want to do and the things you actually end up doing? Do you find your passions, thoughts, and purposes sometimes working against each other? In what ways?

_____

_____

_____

_____

_____

_____

_____

5. Does your heart resonate with Paul's cry to be rescued?

_____

_____

_____

_____

_____

_____

_____

Chapter 6

Rescued Hearts

"Look at them!" squealed the Enemy. "Blaming each other, full of shame, hiding from God! Condemned! Kicked out! These image bearers can no longer fill the earth with glory. If they stand before God, His justice and glory will burn them up. They are left to their own miserable devices, with me in charge of their world! The rule of Satan has begun!

"Wait. What's this? A new plan? Jesus coming to Earth to save these miserable ones? Foolish Father. He just sent His Son into my domain. Apparently, He has forgotten I am in charge here now. One word from me, and I'll have this one killed by the very people He intends to save.

"And now He is dead, buried, and gone to hell. The disciples have gone into hiding. That was the last stand of God; He is defeated forever. God's plans, and the hearts of mankind, are destroyed. All passions, thoughts, and purposes belong to me. Yesssssssss!"

***

47

"Oh, no.

"What happened? This light is killing my eyes. That grave is empty. Jesus is back from hell, and He took so many of my dead with Him! His kingdom is invading my space. And the hearts of the disciples He left on Earth—they are restored, on fire, full of hope and joy and power! My head is crushed, and my power is gone. This world is slipping through my fingers. My deliciously murky kingdom is being invaded by this relentless light."

L et's look at how Paul finished that hopeless-looking verse we read at the end of the last chapter:

> *What an agonizing situation I am in! So who has the power to rescue this miserable man from the unwelcome intruder of sin and death?* ***I give all my thanks to God, for his mighty power has finally provided a way out through our Lord Jesus, the Anointed One!***
>
> (Romans 7:24–25, TPT, emphasis mine)

This is our good news, dear friends. Through His life, death, and resurrection, Jesus offers our hearts freedom from the catastrophic results of the Fall. Many believers, as well as nonbelievers, have a basic understanding of this core message of the gospel. But let's take a minute to review it from the perspective of our hearts.

Let's go back to the garden. There was a split second, a decisive moment, when a dark shroud fell over the hearts of mankind. Adam and Eve's sin—that bite from the tree—changed everything. The light of God's favor was instantly replaced with a black cloud of judgment and doom. God's face turned away from them. They were left at the mercy of the malevolent power of Satan, to whom they had given dominion over the world. Their sentence was death—not the immediate death of the body, but the immediate death of the spirit. That was the end of their hearts' ability to connect with the Source of life, meaning, and purpose. . . forever.

But Wait—There's Hope!

If the solution depended on us, there would be no hope. Our broken hearts cannot fix themselves, cannot redeem themselves, cannot sweet-talk themselves back into relationship with God. But by His grace, God gives each of us *another* chance to choose. The devastation of mankind's hearts was rooted in our choices; God's solution is too.

As we've said before, God is just. He won't give me a wink and declare my sin forgiven. The penalty for sin must be paid, and that penalty is death. If I have to pay that price myself, it's over. I am dead, and my heart is separated from God eternally.

But God sent someone to die my death for me! This someone had to be absolutely sinless, or his death would simply be his own punishment. If this someone had been merely human, he would have had to die for his own sins, not for mine. So, God sent Jesus, His beloved Son, who was not of the earth, and not part of the creation mankind had surrendered to Satan.

Of course, Satan tried to convince Jesus to follow in Adam and Eve's footsteps:

> *Then the devil took him up and revealed to him all the kingdoms of the world in a moment of time. "I will give you the glory of these kingdoms and authority over them," the devil said, "because they are mine to give to anyone I please. I will give it all to you if you will worship me."*
>
> *(Luke 4:5–7, NLT)*

This was the same temptation Satan offered to Adam and Eve: "Ignore God, follow me, and you can be the one in charge!" Jesus did not challenge Satan's claim of authority. He knew Adam and Eve had surrendered dominion to Satan. But Jesus did what Adam and Eve did not do: He refused to give in. He did not sin. He leaned on the Word of God and kept His heart devoted to the Lord as he replied, "The Scriptures say, 'You must worship the LORD your God and serve only him'." (Luke 4:8, NLT)

Jesus had no sin, but He took the sin of mankind on Himself. In place of us, He received the full measure of God's wrath, and His heart endured the separation from God He did not deserve. His blood paid for my sin. He died my death so I can live! My sins became His, and His righteousness became mine. God no longer hides His face from me because He doesn't see any sin when He looks at me. He sees the perfection of Jesus:

> *He Himself bore our sins in His body on the cross, so that we*
> *might die to sin and live to righteousness.*
> *(1 Peter 2:24, NASB)*

> *God made him who had no sin to be sin for us, so that in him*
> *we might become the righteousness of God.*
> *(2 Corinthians 5:21)*

But there's more. Jesus not only died on my behalf and paid the price once and for all, but He also rose from the dead! He is alive *now.* The power of death itself has been broken. I do not have a dead Savior; I have a Savior who is eternally alive. By His death and resurrection, my heart is free from the dominion of Satan—the power of sin—in this life, and the fear of death has no hold on me. Jesus speaks to my heart in triumph: "Don't be afraid! I am the First and the Last. I am the living one. I died, but look—I am alive forever and ever! And I hold the keys of death and the grave." (Revelation 1:17–18, NLT)

Jesus's sacrifice was not the instantaneous magical cure hypothesized earlier. No *poof*, *shazam*, or *voila*. As we said, true relationship is rooted in choice, and this is a relationship we must opt into. And this opting requires faith. Christians are called believers because we have chosen this relationship with *faith*.

Entering into a Life of Faith

Living in relationship with God through faith is a lifelong process with many implications. For one thing, having faith means believing God's assessment of us is true. And is that so hard to believe? God says our hearts were created for relationship with Him, but because of the fallen world, we were born predisposed to ignore Him and want our own way. So, we go through life trying to satisfy our hearts with stuff that leaves us broken and unsatisfied. If we are completely honest with ourselves, that is a fair description of us.

Having agreed with this description, we must believe God's truth about Himself: He exists, He is good, He is absolutely just, and He has good things in store for those who seek Him.

Having faith also means acknowledging that under God's justice, I am worthy only of death and unfit for those good things He has promised. Paul states it clearly in Romans: "All have sinned and fall short of the glory of God" (Romans 3:23), and as we just quoted: "the wages of sin is death." (Romans 6:23)

Then, I must believe Jesus came and did for me what I could not do for myself: "These [things] are written that you may believe that Jesus is the Messiah, the Son of God, and that by believing you may have life in his name." (John 20:31)

So, the penalty for sin has been paid, and my relationship with God can be restored. What is my part? To receive His grace, to confess that my sin makes me worthy of nothing but death, and then by faith to receive Jesus's death as my own. The Bible assures us, "If we confess our sins, he is faithful and just and will forgive us our sins and purify us from all unrighteousness." (1 John 1:9)

Receiving this gift is the beginning of my heart's journey to wholeness. And this part really does happen in an instant. The minute I confess my need and receive His complete work on my behalf, I am forgiven. It is immediate, and it is eternal. My relationship to God is instantly restored. Nothing can ever again come between my heart and its eternal Lover:

> *For I am convinced that neither death nor life, neither angels nor demons, neither the present nor the future, nor any powers, neither height nor depth, nor anything else in all creation, will be able to separate us from the love of God that is in Christ Jesus our Lord.*
>
> *(Romans 8:38–39)*

Before we move forward, take a few minutes to let this truth invade your *inner fountain of passion, thought, and purpose.* Whether you received the gift of salvation today, a year ago, or decades ago, your heart needs to be reminded it has an open door to the heart of God. Always. It doesn't matter whether you can feel it right now. Maybe you've had a bad hair day or it's the wrong time of the month. Maybe you burned dinner. Maybe you had an argument with your husband or you're just plain tired of your kids. Maybe it's been a long time since you opened your Bible or showed up at church. Maybe you've given in to a temptation you thought you had already conquered. You never have to worry God will find you out. He already has. And His loving presence has never left. It never will.

But the story doesn't end here . . .

Chapter 6 Reflection

1. How would you describe the "death" that entered the world in the Garden of Eden?

_____

_____

_____

2. What are some of the specific effects of that "death" in your life?

_____

_____

_____

3. In 2 Corinthians 5:21, quoted in this chapter, the Apostle Paul describes a trade: we give God our sin, He gives us His righteousness. What was the cost of this for Jesus? Why was He willing to pay that price?

_____

_____

_____

4. What are the immediate, eternal benefits that can be yours *right now* as you accept that trade? How would you describe the difference between the one-time act of accepting that trade, and the journey of your heart to wholeness?

_____

_____

_____

Part Three:
Provision for the Journey

Restored Hearts

Satan watched in horror as the gospel continued to spread. The more he opposed it, the more people received the good news.

But then, he had an idea: "What if I actually promote this bad news, but not in its entirety? Maybe just enough to make people feel good? 'Here's your free pass to heaven, and a few rules to live by. But you don't really need to change your life; you can carry on as before. You're golden!' Maybe I could twist it enough to add even more chains to their hearts . . . 'Just be sure to do this and stop doing that, and God will smile on you,' I could tell them. Oh, the hopelessness, the defeat, the futile attempts to please God I could foist upon them! They might be God's kids, but they won't understand the inheritance they have. They will not grasp the utter destruction Jesus has wreaked on my kingdom. My hatred for God and his miserable glory bearers is alive and well."

Yes, Jesus sought us, found us, and saved us. But what about healing and restoration? What about being free from the power of sin? Anyone who has taken that first step of receiving salvation will tell you their hearts weren't instantly healed. Satan was still lying to them, and they were still, to one degree or another, doing things that were wrong and destructive.

The good news is salvation is not limited to the saving of my soul for eternity! The blessings start *now*.

Jesus says of Himself: "The Son of Man has come to seek and to save that which was lost" (Luke 19:10). Sometimes, an English translation of the Greek doesn't say enough. This is one of those places. If we expand that verse to include more of the Greek's shades of meaning for the words "seek" and "lost," it might read something like, "The Son of Man has come to seek, find, save, heal, and restore that which was lost, destroyed, marred, and dead."

Every heart qualifies! Whether we are merely marred or totally lost, destroyed, or dead, we can each confidently bring our hearts to Jesus. We have talked about comfort, and that is part of the process. But neither salvation nor comfort is the final goal for our hearts. Jesus is actively seeking hearts to restore them to Garden-of-Eden wholeness.

The truth is, although salvation immediately restored our fellowship with God and secured our eternity with Him, we are still living in the dark world Adam and Eve relinquished to Satan. Even though Satan has lost the title to our souls, he is deeply committed to our misery and bondage as long as we live on this earth. If he can keep God's children broken, half-hearted, and hopeless, he will diminish our ability to experience God's goodness and fill the earth with His glory.

Satan hopes we will not understand his utter defeat at the cross and the glorious power that has been unleashed in us, through us, and for us. If we have a limited picture of what Jesus has done, our pursuit of Him will be limited. Our expectations will be diminished. If Jesus hasn't taken care of *everything*, then our hopes and expectations will depend on our ability to heal and grow on our own. And we can't do it. To pursue whole hearts, we must know the whole truth.

God's Gift of Salvation

Salvation is often referred to as "receiving Jesus into your heart." This is a useful phrase if taken literally. It's not a token acquiescence to some information that has been presented to us. It is actually choosing to open our *inner fountains of passion, thought, and purpose* to the very presence of the risen Christ.

My little act of faith in my early twenties—accepting the invitation to "Come"—unleashed the all-consuming power of love in my heart. Jesus Himself came to reside there, and He brought the full power of His death and resurrection to tear down walls, heal brokenness, and restore those precious things which had been hidden in my heart since He knit me together in my mother's womb.

Paul prayed the believers in Ephesus would begin to comprehend this love that is beyond comprehension, and which releases the fullness of God in believers' hearts:

> *I kneel before the Father, from whom every family in heaven and on earth derives its name. I pray that out of his glorious riches he may strengthen you with power through his Spirit in your inner being, so that Christ may dwell in your hearts through faith. And I pray that you, being rooted and established in love, may have power, together with all the Lord's holy people, to grasp how wide and long and high and deep is the love of Christ, and to know this love that surpasses knowledge—that you may be filled to the measure of all the fullness of God.*
>
> *(Ephesians 3:14–19)*

Paul was so moved by the reality of what he just wrote and prayed for the Ephesians, he broke out in worship, right in the middle of his letter to them!

> *Now to him who is able to do immeasurably more than all we ask or imagine, according to his power that is at work within us, to him be glory in the church and in Christ Jesus throughout all generations, for ever and ever! Amen.*
>
> *(Ephesians 3:20–21)*

When I look back at that glorious day over forty years ago, I am astonished and appalled at how self-centered, naïve, and rebellious I was. I was engaged in activities and attitudes that I had no idea were ruinous to my own heart and to the hearts around me. As the Lord invited me into fellowship with Him and as I opened myself to His Word, I gradually became aware of the utter desolation within me. My *passions, thoughts, and purposes* were in terrible disarray. Satan loved it, the world was patting me on the back, my heart was shut down, and I had no idea who I was.

I am so thankful Jesus never gave up on me! My eternity with Him was secured the day I accepted His invitation, but He did not want me, nor does He want any of us, to limp through our earthly lives with smiles painted on our faces. He bought us more than eternity with Him. He purchased our healing and restoration. (I'm using "restoration" to refer to the process of making our hearts whole.) He has made His overcoming power available to us. We have access to all the resources necessary to walk in wholeness.

We need a reality check here. As we've said, our *salvation* is a one-time occurrence, after which our eternity is secure. We belong to Jesus forever! However, our *restoration* is not a destination, but a journey. The goal is to become mature—completely Christlike—but that won't happen until we see Him face to face. Restoration is the process. Jesus's invitation to come is both an invitation to be with Him in eternity *and* to become more and more like Him along the way.

Those of us who want to pursue whole hearts must keep on choosing to say yes to this invitation. It is not a yes to a list of things to do, but a yes to following Him where He takes us. It is a yes to placing our hearts in His hands and trusting His leadership.

Satan wants to trick us into thinking Jesus has a to-do list for us to check off so we stay in His good graces. Our Enemy offers us a self-help scam that depends on our own resources. "Get the right program and follow it well. And *then*," Satan would have us believe, "you can be good enough to please God and deserve help from Him." That is *not* good news! But we are tempted to buy into it because something in us hates embracing our weakness and vulnerability.

We can embrace our brokenness and helplessness only because our loving Father has promised to walk with us and to give us the grace to move forward not in our own strength, but in His:

> *By his divine power, God has given us everything we need for living a godly [wholehearted] life. We have received all of this by coming to know him, the one who called us to himself by means of his marvelous glory and excellence. And because of his glory and excellence, he has given us great and precious promises. These are the promises that enable you to share his divine nature and escape the world's corruption caused by human desires.*
>
> *(2 Peter 1:3–4, NLT)*

God has given us His promises because of His glory and excellence— *His* glory and excellence, not ours. The promises are a gift, not a reward. The grace of God will meet us in every aspect of our need.

Grace is the favor of God. It is freely given, neither bought nor earned. Grace fuels our restoration. Grace enables our mustard-seed faith to keep saying yes to the Father. Grace overcomes our hard-headed, brokenhearted approach to life.

To take full advantage of this grace available to us, we must know the truth about ourselves, the world, and God. The journey of restoration is a journey of revelation. The more we know of our need, the more we will press into Jesus's provision. The more we know of that provision, the more we will ask. The more we ask, the more we will experience. Jesus said, "Then you will know the truth, and the truth will set you free." (John 8:32)

The journey into restoration is a journey into truth.

Chapter 7 Reflection

1. Jesus bought us more than an eternal future with Him. He came to seek, find, save, heal, and restore that which was lost, destroyed, marred, and dead. How does your heart respond to this truth? What needs or desires does it awaken in your heart?

_____

_____

_____

_____

2. After reading this chapter, how would you define "receiving Jesus into your heart"? What are some of His roles there? What is your response to allowing Him those roles?

_____

_____

_____

_____

3. How would you define grace? What appeals to your heart about it?

_____

_____

_____

_____

4. Are there areas where you can see you have been deceived about the extent of your own brokenness?

_____

_____

_____

_____

_____

_____

5. Have you been deceived about the extent of God's mercy, love, and grace?

_____

_____

_____

_____

_____

_____

_____

Chapter 8

Hearts Gripped by Truth

"I love the twenty-first century!" said Satan. "Time and technology have been my friends. God keeps promoting ways to dispense His truth, but I can find ways to pervert them all! Way back when Gutenberg was crafting his press for the express purpose of printing the Bible, I was envisioning a printing industry I could use to dispense my deception, confusion, and filth. And now look! I can spread lies and destruction around the globe in seconds!

"God gave those image bearers a disturbing ability to learn and understand. He even gave them the creativity to build more and better equipment, all to get a greater picture of the vast wisdom and power and magnitude of the Father who created it all. Ha! I have twisted their awe into arrogance. Instead of understanding that their ability even to think comes from being made in His image, they think their greatness is a result of their own effort.

"And their broken hearts? Well, I have them working on ever-more creative ways to hide and blame and medicate and

ignore. 'Here,' I whisper, 'Read this, take this, try this. You can take care of your own heart.'"

In his letters, the Apostle Paul addresses the need of our hearts to know truth. In his second letter to Timothy, he describes the days we live in:

> *But mark this: There will be terrible times in the last days. People will be lovers of themselves, lovers of money, boastful, proud, abusive, disobedient to their parents, ungrateful, unholy, without love, unforgiving, slanderous, without self-control, brutal, not lovers of the good, treacherous, rash, conceited, lovers of pleasure rather than lovers of God—having a form of godliness but denying its power. Have nothing to do with such people.*
>
> *(2 Timothy 3:1–5)*

This description of the last days perfectly reflects the times we are living in right now. We do not know how much longer Jesus will tarry, but we must be aware of the prevalent and destructive dangers to our hearts. There are those who practice and promote godless living, and they must not be allowed influence in our hearts.

Let's continue, starting with the last sentence of the above passage:

> *Have nothing to do with such people. They are the kind who worm their way into homes and gain control over gullible women, who are loaded down with sins and are swayed by all kinds of evil desires, always learning but never able to come to a knowledge of the truth.*
>
> *(2 Timothy 3:5–7)*

Here Paul is admonishing Timothy, who is leading the young church in Ephesus, to remove the influence of those who are promoting godless living. Avoid them. And he gives us one reason why—because of the danger they bring to certain women. *Women!* That could be you or me.

Why would Paul caution Timothy to guard specifically the women from this influence? Well, I can think of two good reasons to guard something: because it is valuable, and because it is vulnerable.

Valuable? Yes! Women are precious to God, and they carry incredible value that must be protected and nurtured for the increase of God's kingdom and the spread of His glory.

Vulnerable? For sure. Paul was addressing a particular problem in ancient Ephesus, a city committed to pagan cults, the goddess Artemis, and perverse sexual rituals. These cults, which appeared to promote women, actually encouraged them to assume attitudes and activities destructive to their hearts and their society. We don't hear much about Artemis these days, but there will always be false teachings that distort our identities and lead us astray. None of us is immune. And Paul says the gullible women are the ones who are "always learning, but never able to come to a knowledge of the truth." Paul tasked Timothy with keeping deceptive influences away from the church, but there is something we can personally participate in: Come to a knowledge of the truth!

Rejecting Error, Embracing Truth

It is important for us to avoid the pitfalls of uninformed, impulsive hearts. We can take in a lot of information—processing it, categorizing it, memorizing it, even teaching it—and still be weak, weighed down, and impulsive. We must do more than just learn stuff; we must come to the knowledge of the truth. Truth must get beyond our brains; it must have a home in our hearts.

We women have a marvelous yet frustrating capacity to act purely from emotion, even when our brains are telling us not to! Our *inner fountains of passion, thought, and purpose* must be gripped by truth, or they may give in to destructive lies and temptations.

Our hearts have been rescued, but they are not yet whole. To gain and maintain whole hearts, it is imperative that we come to a confident, transformative knowledge of the truth.

We will be looking at many aspects of truth for our journey, but they're all rooted in the core truth we unlocked in the previous chapter:

> *So now I live with the confidence that there is nothing in the universe that can separate us from God's love. I'm convinced that his love will triumph over death, life's troubles, fallen angels, or dark rulers in the heavens. There is nothing in our present or future circumstances that can weaken his love. There is no power above us or beneath us—no power that could ever be found in the universe that can distance us from God's passionate love, which is lavished on us through our Lord Jesus, the Anointed One!*
>
> (Romans 8:38–39, TPT) •

This is the truth: you are loved by a Father who will never leave you.

Your hope is in the fact that the God of the universe is committed to your whole heart. All His power is on your side as you embark on this journey. Your wayward steps and stupid mistakes will never move Him to give up on you.

As our hearts are gripped by the truth of God's love, our passions and purposes will begin to change. What begins as a mere desire to know and follow God's ways takes root and begins to engage the way we think and act as well. The chasm between what God has promised and what we are actually experiencing will begin to bother us. We will become increasingly aware of how *unlike* Jesus we are. We will recognize a need and a desire for more of everything good in us, through us, and for us.

This is the work of Jesus, drawing us to a life of restoration and transformation. It includes comfort, healing for the pain, disarming the lies, and experiencing more and more of Jesus as our hearts' Lover. "Transformation" refers to the outer working of this inner restoration—the process of becoming more and more like Him.

We will need—and long for—more truth. In this Information Age, our minds are constantly bombarded with "wisdom" that is foolishness and "solutions" that just trade one misery for another. The Bible tells us transformation is dependent on rejecting worldly wisdom and renewing our minds through the knowledge of God's ways:

> *Do not conform to the pattern of this world, but be transformed by the renewing of your mind. Then you will be able to test and approve what God's will is—his good, pleasing and perfect will.*
>
> *(Romans 12:2)*

As our hearts come to a knowledge of the truth, there will be an opportunity to respond to that truth. Transformation is dependent on knowing the truth *and* acting on it. Our restored hearts will help us here. Our passions and purposes will begin to conform to God's passions and purposes for us, and our hungry hearts will respond to the wisdom of God's ways.

No Strings Attached

I want to be careful not to paint a picture of God as one who is requiring us to accomplish something to win His favor. He does not throw a bunch of requirements at us and then stand back to see if we'll obey. He is not withholding His love from us until we meet His expectations. No, we are *already* residents of His kingdom because of the blood of Jesus. We have unlimited access to His love and goodness.

When I was just beginning my own journey, there was nothing I could do to earn more of God's love. He had already given it all. But my pitiful little broken heart had to heal and grow to experience greater depths of His love and to bring that love to my broken world. I *still* have a lot of healing and growing to do.

We are invited to partner with God by choosing to say yes to His ways and His plans for our lives. We are invited to engage in the battle against the lies and temptations of the Enemy. We are invited to pursue a knowledge of the truth.

In his letter to the first-century church, James counsels us that transformation requires both hearing *and* doing. We must let God's ways reveal our own foolishness and weakness. And we must let that revelation motivate us to obedience. He writes:

> But don't just listen to God's word. You must do what it says. Otherwise, you are only fooling yourselves. For if you listen to the word and don't obey, it is like glancing at your face in a mirror. You see yourself, walk away, and forget what you look like.
>
> (James 1:22–24, NLT)

James provides a great analogy for us women. How many of us look in the mirror and just walk away without taking a second to adjust *something*? If the mirror shows us something out of place, we do something about it! God has provided His Word as a mirror for us. It is a gift, not a ball and chain. It is our handbook for caring for our hearts and the hearts of others. His Word shows us where a thought or action or attitude is out of whack or downright destructive. We can choose to walk away and forget about it, or we can make some adjustments. When it comes to our looks, we see our disheveled reflection in the mirror and choose to make some changes. For transformation, we must likewise let God's

Word reveal our foolish ways and inspire us to ask Him to help us think and respond differently.

We do not know enough to govern our own lives. The writer of Proverbs says it clearly (and repeats it a couple chapters later for good measure): "There is a path before each person that *seems* right, but it ends in death." (Proverbs 14:12; 16:25, NLT, emphasis mine)

The Apostle Peter instructs us to set aside our naïve ways and long for the truth that will help us grow. He says this longing will come from hearts that have experienced the goodness of God:

> *So abandon every form of evil, deceit, hypocrisy, feelings of jealousy and slander. In the same way that nursing infants cry for milk, you must intensely crave the pure spiritual milk of God's Word. For this "milk" will cause you to grow into maturity, fully nourished and strong for life especially now that you have had a taste of the goodness of Yahweh and have experienced his kindness.*
>
> *(1 Peter 2:1-3, TPT)*

As our hearts are being restored, as we taste the kindness of the Lord, we will find ourselves gradually being motivated to adjust our lives according to His Word. As we know and understand what is true, as our identities and purposes come into focus, and as our love and trust in God grow, our desire to know and act on the truth will increase: "For God is working in you, giving you the desire and the power to do what pleases him." (Philippians 2:13, NLT)

As we continue to journey together, I pray you will experience restoration and transformation in your life. I mean that literally: I am praying for our Father to pierce the lies that have held you back and renew how you think about yourself. I pray He will empower you with new conviction, new hope, and new vision for your life. I pray your heart will be touched at the deepest level. No matter where you are on your journey, there's more of everything good available to you!

Early in His ministry, Jesus read a prophecy from Isaiah 61 and boldly claimed it to be about Himself:

> *On the Sabbath day he went into the synagogue, as was his custom. He stood up to read, and the scroll of the prophet Isaiah was handed to him. Unrolling it, he found the place where it is written: "The Spirit of the Lord is on me, because he has anointed me to proclaim good news to the poor. He has sent me to proclaim freedom for the prisoners and recovery of sight for the blind, to set the oppressed free, to proclaim the year of the Lord's favor." Then he rolled up the scroll, gave it back to the attendant and sat down. The eyes of everyone in the synagogue were fastened on him. He began by saying to them, "Today this scripture is fulfilled in your hearing.*
>
> *(Luke 4:16–21)*

Scripture *has* been fulfilled! Freedom, vision, and favor for *our* hearts! Thank you, Lord, for truth that sets us free.

Chapter 8 Reflection

1. In what ways do you see yourself as "valuable"? "Vulnerable"?

_____

_____

_____

2. Have you been a pursuer of truth? In what ways does truth inform your passions? Thoughts? Purposes?

_____

_____

_____

3. As you embark on this journey, how confident are you that nothing can separate you from the love of God that is in Christ Jesus? Is your heart gripped by this truth? How is it affecting your thoughts and purposes?

_____

_____

_____

4. I suggest that the Bible is a gift, not a ball and chain. How have you perceived the Bible as one or the other of those?

_____

_____

_____

_____

Chapter 9

Your Heart's Companion

"This is a disaster for me," lamented Satan at Pentecost. "The disciples saw Jesus resurrected from the dead and risen to be with His Father; I ended up having to relinquish that ground. But I was hoping to keep the Holy Spirit under wraps. I wanted the disciples to see Jesus as merely a good teacher and friend who had been taken away from them."

Jesus had told the disciples to wait—Satan loved it when He said that! It was the perfect moment to move in and bring fear and doubt. And so far, the disciples seemed to be following the game plan. They locked themselves behind closed doors, afraid to be seen in public, waiting for a god who was apparently in no hurry to show up. Three years of relationship with Jesus, experiencing His love, doing miracles with Him . . . their hearts had fond memories and some new rules to live by. Hopefully they would be content with that.

And then—blam! Howling wind! Tongues of fire! The chatter of unknown languages! That unpredictable, Jesus-

denying Peter leapt up and preached as if He were God Himself! Those impotent disciples became anointed powerhouses of miracles, preaching, healing, and wisdom. The very Spirit and Presence of Jesus came and invaded their hearts.

"This is loathsome to me," said Satan. "But I have a new plan. I will make this Holy Spirit loathsome to people as well. I can energize that spirit of independence—which I personally released over the world, pat my back—to make all this supernatural stuff offensive. Let Jesus be a nice friend who will be waiting for some people when they die. Let Him make His invasive suggestions about how they should live. But they will never surrender themselves to this power they cannot understand or control. They must not."

I n the following chapters, we will look at what God says is true about our hearts and our lives. As we look to our hearts' handbook, the Bible, we may find ourselves both challenged and encouraged. We may react with fear, doubt, or confusion. Do not be dismayed by the intensity of the battle or by your own weaknesses or failures. You have an Enemy who is fully invested in your broken heart, but God's Word will dismantle his influence and destruction.

In this journey toward a transforming knowledge of the truth, it is important to know your heart is not alone. In fact, an unredeemed heart is utterly unable to undertake this journey on its own. Satan's opposition to whole hearts dominates every aspect of this fallen world.

By God's grace, your heart can stay engaged and keep choosing. Your failures will never remove you from God's love, and even failed attempts, when touched by His grace, can move you forward in strength and healing. Your heart *is* being restored. You *are* being transformed. And you are not left to your own devices for even the smallest step. Jesus has given us supernatural help for this process.

The Holy Spirit, Our Helper

Jesus's death and resurrection had a purpose we haven't discussed yet. In John 16:7, He says to His disciples, "But very truly I tell you, it is for your good that I am going away. Unless I go away, the Counselor will not come to you; but if I go, I will send him to you."

When Jesus was alive on the earth, His presence was limited to one place at a time. If you wanted to see Him, if you wanted a touch from Him, if you wanted to ask Him a question, you had to find out where He was and hope you could get to Him through the crowds.

But He promised that after His death and resurrection, He would send another Helper. This Helper is also referred to as the Teacher, Advocate, Comforter, and Counselor. . . Jesus was talking about His own Spirit, the Holy Spirit! And the Spirit of Jesus is not floating around "out there" somewhere. The Spirit comes to reside *in our hearts*, as we see in 2 Corinthians 1:21-22: "He anointed us, set his seal of ownership on us, and put his Spirit in our hearts as a deposit, guaranteeing what is to come." Likewise, Romans 5:5 says, "God's love has been poured out into our hearts through the Holy Spirit, who has been given to us."

This is good news for our hearts! The Holy Spirit—the Spirit of Jesus—has taken up residence in us! We have Him with us all the time, and He can work from the inside out.

I cannot overstate the value of the person of the Holy Spirit in your journey toward wholeness. Jesus told His disciples the Holy Spirit would lead them to truth: "But the Advocate, the Holy Spirit, whom the Father will send in my name, will teach you all things and will remind you of everything I have said to you." (John 14:26)

After His resurrection, Jesus admonished His disciples to wait for the promised Holy Spirit before they began their ministry:

> *On one occasion, while he was eating with them, he gave them this command: "Do not leave Jerusalem, but wait for the gift*

my Father promised, which you have heard me speak about.
For John baptized with water, but in a few days you will be
baptized with the Holy Spirit."

(Acts 1:4-5)

Jesus ascended into heaven after speaking those words to His disciples. And 10 days later, on the Jewish holy day of Pentecost, the Holy Spirit was poured out as promised. Those first disciples received a transformative supernatural anointing for their ministry. For example, Peter, who less than two weeks earlier had fearfully denied (three times!) even knowing Jesus, stood up and preached the gospel, boldly calling people to repent. Three thousand disciples were added that day! (see Acts 2:41) The Church was born.

Later, when Paul encountered new believers at Ephesus, He wanted to make sure they had received the Holy Spirit:

While Apollos was at Corinth, Paul took the road through the
interior and arrived at Ephesus. There he found some disciples
and asked them, "Did you receive the Holy Spirit when you
believed?" They answered, "No, we have not even heard that
there is a Holy Spirit."

(Acts 19:1-2)

The Holy Spirit is promised to every believer, and God is faithful in all His promises. Paul was not asking the Ephesian believers if God had *given* them the Spirit when they believed. Of course, He had. It was His promise. Paul was asking if they had *received* the Spirit. Receiving, welcoming, acknowledging, taking hold of—these are appropriate, *active* responses to something that has been given.

When I order my old-lady supplements, Amazon does a pretty good job of fulfilling their promise to deliver them. A package arrives on my front porch, and I even get a photo proving it was delivered. But if I do not actually unlock my door, pick up the package, open it, and follow the directions, those supplements do not help me. I cannot blame Amazon. I cannot blame the supplements. I cannot claim I've taken those supplements. The supplements may have been given to me, but unless I choose to open that box, I have not *received* them.

This is a trite example, but the point is applicable. The Father pours His Holy Spirit into our hearts when we become believers. But the Spirit will not force His way into our lives. Jesus invites us to welcome the Spirit and allow Him complete access to our *inner fountains of passion, thought, and purpose.* We are invited to welcome the supernatural power and wisdom that enables us to heal and grow.

As a believer, it is possible to keep God at arm's length, acknowledging Him without inviting Him to invade our lives. Humans tend to fear or distrust anything we cannot control or explain. But isn't that exactly what we need? We cannot explain the woundedness in our hearts. We do not have a natural path to wholeness. We need this Counselor, this Helper, this Comforter and Teacher, to lead us on a supernatural journey.

How to Walk with the Spirit

Ladies, do not leave the Father's gift of the Holy Spirit on the doorstep of your heart. If you have not already done so, I encourage you to take time to receive Him. Acknowledge Him. Welcome Him. Invite Him into the depths of your heart with His supernatural wisdom and power. Talk to Him and ask Him to talk to you. He is a faithful Friend.

I invite you to contend for your wholeness. As you take this journey with the Spirit, here are some tools I have found useful in ensuring my learning actually transforms my heart:

1. **Don't be in a hurry.**

   Transformation is a process, and it takes time. Be aware of what the Holy Spirit is saying to you. Let Him speak His deep secrets to you. Let Him reveal your own deep secrets. Expose your life to Him. Talk to Him about it. Pray about it. Meditate on it.

We live in a microwave world where everyone expects speedy gratification. The sense of actually working toward a long-term goal is being lost in our world. But we are a people who are both building and being built. We are waiting and growing, watching and becoming. We must set our hearts and minds on the steady, long-term advance of the kingdom in our hearts and in our world. "And we all, who with unveiled faces contemplate the Lord's glory, are being transformed into his image with ever-increasing glory, which comes from the Lord, who is the Spirit." (2 Corinthians 3:18)

2. **Repent joyfully and often.**

As the Holy Spirit opens your eyes to the passions, thoughts, and purposes contrary to God's redemptive plan for your life, embrace repentance as a gift. Learn to discern whose voice is correcting you. The correction of the Holy Spirit will bring godly sorrow and awaken a desire to change. Satan's accusations will heap on shame, condemnation, and hopelessness. Paul puts it this way: "Godly sorrow brings repentance that leads to salvation and leaves no regret, but worldly sorrow brings death." (2 Corinthians 7:10)

Repentance is one of the most powerful tools we have. Don't be afraid to discover and acknowledge that you have been arrogant, bitter, gullible, offended, untruthful, blind, weak, afraid, or just plain wrong. You *have* been. I have been. It is a privilege and a joy to get to repent of those things and break their power over us.

If the Holy Spirit shows you how your beliefs, attitudes, or actions have been contrary to God's plan for you, take time to confess to Him. Confession simply means agreeing with God's judgment about something. Take time to articulate the areas where God has showed you your error. And take time to receive the forgiveness Jesus purchased for you with his life. That thing you just confessed was laid on Jesus over two thousand years ago. He carried it, so you don't have to any more. Put it in His hands, let the redemptive power of His blood cover it, and let it go!

In the New Testament, the Greek word for "repentance" indicates a change in one's thinking. Proclaim your desire, by God's grace, to think and act differently. Press into His grace, knowing you cannot change on your own. God knows your weakness. The same grace that brought you to the place where you could see and confess your sin will also give you the power to overcome it. This whole process starts and finishes with Him. The Holy Spirit will walk alongside you, teaching, comforting, counseling, and reminding you of the Father who loves you: "He who began a good work in you will carry it on to completion until the day of Christ Jesus." (Philippians 1:6)

Repentance shuts the door on the Enemy and opens us to healing and new life. It taps us into the power of the Cross. It makes us eligible for everything Jesus bought for us. The Cross is not just about getting a free pass to heaven. It's about the right and the power to be whole.

You may find yourself revisiting old habits and thought patterns, but they do not define you! Let confession and repentance be quick, joyful, and full of faith. You are simply asking the Lord to apply His gift to your area of need: "Oh, drat, I did it again, Lord. Thank You that forgiveness is mine and You are at work transforming me. I receive Your grace and trust You to transform my *inner fountain of passion, thought, and purpose* as only You can do." Do not wallow in self-pity. Do not receive the guilt and shame the Enemy will keep offering you. You are free to get up and get on with your life!

3. **Do not wait for someone else to change first.**

You may be living or working in a difficult or oppressive situation. Perhaps it's your husband, your boss, your pastor, a friend, or a parent. There are things those people need to hear, too. But neither you nor I can change them. We must cultivate our own inner lives and respond to Jesus about our own sins without making it dependent on what the significant people in our lives are doing.

My heart goes out to the many women suffering at the hands of those who should be a blessing to them. God knows your pain; He has walked through suffering Himself. If you are in a situation that endangers you or your children, please get help. You are not called to live a life of abuse. If you need to get yourself to a safe place, please start there. But know that you, too, will have your own internal stuff to walk through. May you continue to experience the healing and transforming power of the Spirit!

4. **Connect to other believers.**

A woman alone is very, very vulnerable to the lies of the Enemy, the temptations of the world, and the vicissitudes of her own body and emotions. Other believers have gifts you need. You do not have everything you need apart from them. You cannot grow into who you were created to be without being active in the body of Christ. You need to hear from others, and they need to hear from you. Be a part of a local church. And be a part of a small group of women where you have the freedom and the trust to speak into each other's lives.

This is not a process of gritting your teeth and striving to be something you are not. This is an invitation to walk with the God who loves you and to open your heart to His Holy Spirit. You cannot do it alone. A whole heart and a transformed life are the fruit of walking with Jesus:

> *"I am the vine; you are the branches. If you remain in me and I in you, you will bear much fruit; apart from me you can do nothing."*
>
> *(John 15:5)*

And this promised fruit is exactly what our hearts are looking for:

> *The Holy Spirit produces this kind of fruit in our lives: love, joy, peace, patience, kindness, goodness, faithfulness, gentleness, and self-control. There is no law against these things!*
>
> *(Galatians 5:22-23, NLT)*

Is your heart looking for joy? Has peace evaded you? Do you long for a heart that mirrors Jesus's heart? There is no law against these things! They are the promised outcome of receiving the work of the Holy Spirit in your heart.

Chapter 9 Reflection

1. The Holy Spirit has been called Teacher, Advocate, Comforter, and Counselor. In what ways would you benefit from having these things residing *in your heart*?

_____

_____

_____

_____

_____

2. In what ways have you feared, resisted, or misunderstood the supernatural work of the Holy Spirit?

_____

_____

_____

_____

_____

3. Is repentance difficult for you? Why or why not? Why and how can repentance be joyful?

_____

_____

_____

_____

_____

4. In what areas have you been waiting for someone else to change first?

_____

_____

_____

_____

_____

5. Can you identify areas where you have been gritting your teeth and trying to change on your own?

_____

_____

_____

_____

6. What is the value of sharing your heart's journey with another?

_____

_____

_____

_____

_____

Part Four:
Identity

Chapter 10

The Heart of a Woman

My mother was a woman. My dad was a man. My brothers were boys. My sister and I were girls. And that's about all the thought I gave to gender as a little kid.

What did it mean to be a girl who would grow up to be a woman? I don't remember ever wondering about it. The first time I remember thinking about the fact that I was a girl was in junior high. That was when I became aware that being a girl at that time closed some doors for me. My thoughts had nothing of the deep "Who am I?" contemplations. It was all about "What do I want to do?" I was just focused on what I wanted to do. The thoughts were naïve, shallow, superficial, and self-centered—kind of like most young teenagers' thoughts.

If questions about purpose and identity remain at the superficial and self-centered level, they can lead to confused and destructive answers and choices. My young adulthood was a perfect example. Oh, to have had a God's-eye view of myself! To have known I'd been knit together in my mother's womb by a God who loved me and had eternal plans and purposes for me! That would have changed everything!

A huge part of what we experience is wrapped up in the fact that we were born women. Yours is a woman's heart. It lives in a woman's body. You didn't choose it. Your parents didn't choose it. Before you were born, before anything good or bad happened to you, before you were able to make any choices about life, something very basic was chosen for you by God Himself. He is the only one who can answer our questions about womanhood.

In Chapter 4, we looked at the creation story. God created a world for mankind, and then He created Adam. In Hebrew, *adam* is a generic term for mankind. Only later did it become the given name of the first male. God created humanity first as a single creature. Both male and female were represented in Adam: "So God created mankind [Adam] in His image; in the image of God He created them; male and female He created them" (Genesis 1:27).

Hello, Gorgeous!

And then woman was taken from Adam. It is easy to read quickly through this story and make suppositions about the appearance of woman. But if we take time to read the step-by-step account, a clear picture emerges. Woman was not a copy-and-paste duplicate of Adam, nor did God form her from a different clump of earth. *All* of mankind—male and female—were present in Adam. And then woman was *taken from* Adam. God took part of the substance of Adam and formed it into a woman.

Adam was no longer the same! Part of him had been removed. The woman was made of the same stuff as Adam. She had the same imprint of God on her. She carried the same purpose of being fruitful and multiplying, exercising dominion over the earth, loving God, and filling the earth with His glory. Mankind was separated into two parts, each carrying different revelations of the nature of God.

What about this woman? Exactly when did she show up? And why?

We don't have to do a huge theological study on the word "woman." We don't have to find and compare a bunch of scriptures. We don't have to consult the prophets among us or spend hours in meditative prayer. We can take out our Bibles and start reading from the beginning, and within a few minutes, we have our answer: "It is not good for the man to be alone" (Genesis 2:18).

There. That's it. For the first time in all God's creating, He said, "It is *not* good." Woman was brought forth from man because it was not good for the man to be alone.

God was not surprised by this revelation. He did not bring forth Eve to rectify a mistake. Creation was in process, and He already knew all the steps He would take. Male and female were both represented in Adam, but it was not good for the image of God to exist as a lone creature. God wasn't finished.

Why was it not good for the man to be alone? Because he was to bear the image of God, and *God Himself* is by nature not alone.

God exists eternally as the Trinity: Father, Son, and Holy Spirit. God did not create mankind because He was lonely, or because He needed fellowship. Fellowship already existed in the Godhead before He began creating (in referring to the "Godhead," I mean the Trinity—God in three Persons, including God the Father, God the Son, and God the Holy Spirit). In fact, within the Godhead, creating was a family activity:

*In the beginning **God** created the heavens and the earth.*
(Genesis 1:1, emphasis mine)

*Now the earth was formless and empty, darkness was over the surface of the deep, and the **Spirit of God** was hovering over the waters.*
(Genesis 1:2, emphasis mine)

*In the beginning was the **Word [Jesus]**, and the Word was with God, and the Word was God. He was with God in the* *beginning. Through him all things were made; without him nothing was made that has been made.*

(John 1:1–3, emphasis mine)

Father, Son, and Holy Spirit are all God. Each is different in form and function, but each is God. Together, in relationship with each other, they display the nature of God, which is love. Think about it: the word "love" actually has no meaning outside relationship. We were created to bear the image of God, which means we were created to love. As love is displayed in heaven, so it must be displayed on the earth.

To reflect the image of God, a person must have another being made of the same stuff, and yet separate from himself. Nothing in creation would do. All the animals were brought to Adam, and he named them. But not one of them was a suitable co-lover and co-image bearer. Nothing else in creation could connect with Adam to model and display the interaction that exists in the heavenly Godhead. Fellowship, relationship, unity, honor, intimacy, celebrating each other . . . *love.*

We are not talking about romantic or sexual love. Those aspects of love are awesome, but they do not exist in the Godhead. We are talking about a self-sacrificing, honoring, caring, serving love. It's what separates us from the rest of creation. The angels should look at us on the earth and recognize the kind of love they see in the Godhead.

And what about the rest of God's mandate for Adam, to be fruitful and multiply, filling the earth with the glory of God? God has wisely ordained that it takes two to reproduce. Parenting, loving, working, and ruling the earth: all these are effectively carried out only as we reflect the Godhead in unity, collaboration, and serving each other. Adam could not bear the image of God alone. He needed another—not to meet his personal needs, but to fulfill mankind's purpose.

So, God brought forth the woman.

What Do You Mean, "Helper?"

Now the LORD God said, "It is not good (sufficient, satisfactory) that the man should be alone; I will make him a helper meet (suitable, adapted, complementary) for him."

(Genesis 2:18, AMPC)

Historically, the biblical description of woman as a "helper" has been tragically distorted. Taken out of context, it can create a picture of a secondary character introduced to assist and promote the major character, man. But this helper is not an afterthought. It is not the little helper my granddaughter likes to be in the kitchen. It is not the helper my husband hires to mow the lawn so he has time for more important stuff. It is not an apprentice, or a backup, or a stagehand. This is an essential, indispensable counterpart. Creation is incomplete without her.

Man by himself is not the major character. In fact, man and woman together are not the main characters! The main character is God, and His image is reflected in man and woman *together*.

Nowhere in Scripture is *ezer*, the Hebrew word for helper, used to describe a useful but inferior companion. In fact, this term is most often used to describe God!

*We wait in hope for the LORD; he is our **help** [ezer] and our shield.*

(Psalm 33:20, emphasis mine)

*But as for me, I am poor and needy; come quickly to me, O God. You are my **help** [ezer] and my deliverer; LORD, do not delay.*

(Psalm 70:5, emphasis mine)

You are destroyed, Israel, because you are against me, against
*your **helper** [ezer].*

(Hosea 13:9, emphasis mine)

This helper (*ezer*) is described in Hebrew as *neged*, which can be translated as "meet, just right, suitable, fit for, corresponding to, and 'as his counterpart.'" The Hebrew actually means "in front of, opposite, or corresponding to." That is what was required! Another human being, separate from and complementary to Adam, face to face and side by side, to fulfill in unity the destiny of mankind. In their relating to each other, God's image would be displayed on the earth.

God commanded mankind, "Be fruitful and increase in number; fill the earth and subdue it" (Genesis 1:28). It was interesting for me to discover the Hebrew word in this verse for "fill" can also be translated "consecrate." If I rephrased this verse considering Genesis 1:26 ("Let us make man in our image, to reign over the whole earth"), I would offer this paraphrase of Genesis 1:28:

> *God blessed them and said to them, "Allow more and more of*
> *the image of God to grow in you. As you love each other, as you*
> *raise kids who carry My image, and as your expanding family*
> *carries My image throughout the earth, the earth itself will be*
> *consecrated and made to conform to My purposes."*

God gave mankind—man and woman together—dominion over all that was created before them. We have a mandate to love God first, and then, in relationship with Him and with each other, we can fill the rest of creation, making it conform to His purposes and making it a display of His glory. Man cannot do it alone, and woman cannot do it alone. God never intended for us to do it alone. Alone is *not good*.

God's plan and purpose in creation should fill us with wonder, humility, and holy fear as we take our places among men and women in filling the earth with the knowledge of God. Our hearts, our *inner fountains of passion, thought, and purpose*, must be healthy and fully engaged. Broken, deceived hearts and everything that flows from them paralyze us and hinder God's purposes.

We are image bearers! There is a call on us as women to take God at His word and be all He created us to be. In this broken world, it is tempting at times to lament being a woman, lament having a holy purpose, and even lament having a heart to deal with! But God's purposes are full of love and truth, and He is deeply committed to restoring our hearts according to His glorious image. We *can* move forward with absolute confidence He will lead us and bless us on this journey to whole hearts.

Chapter 10 Reflection

1. Have there been times when you have lamented being a woman? Why?

_____

_____

_____

_____

_____

_____

2. Why is it important to get a true Biblical perspective on womanhood? What are the things that have opposed and twisted that perspective?

_____

_____

_____

_____

_____

_____

_____

Chapter 11

The Heart of a Queen . . .

I grew up in the desert. Reno, Nevada, to be exact. Reno was small in those days—about 35,000 people, and lots of wind and dust. Metropolitan, it was not. It had the outdated aura of the Wild West. The place was notorious for quick no-fault divorces and legalized gambling, with a well-known brothel less than twenty miles away. "Reno-ite" was not something I would have been proud to put on a resume if I had been thinking about that at the time. Nothing there inspired me toward a future. Does anything good come from Reno?

My mom's family, I learned later, was actually well known in social circles in Reno, but the family didn't spend much effort knowing each other. My grandparents lived in the same town, but I remember seeing them only a handful of times a year. I derived no sense of identity or significance from my family.

After my folks divorced, my dad moved his new family (which included me) twice in two years. I attended three different high schools in three different states within a period of two and a half years. I still have never been to a high school class reunion because I never identified with a high school class. I had nothing significant I identified with. The concept of identity eluded me completely.

Celebrating the Truth of Who We Are

Part of restoring our hearts to wholeness is knowing and celebrating the truth about who we really are. Our hearts are diminished or enlarged depending on what we believe about ourselves. How we see ourselves colors how we interpret our circumstances. Our sense of identity has the power to open our eyes to opportunities, or to blind us to them. Identity influences how we feel about ourselves, how we relate to the world around us, and how we approach God.

Who or what have you given the right to define you? Who or what informs your *inner fountain of passion, thought, and purpose* about its significance?

We all have been influenced by what the important people in our lives have said to and about us. We have taken to heart how we have been treated. Both our successes and our failures speak to us about our identities. We evaluate ourselves by the things we do, the things we don't do, and the things that happen to us. To one degree or another, we allow these things to define our value and our purpose.

Let's explore the concept of identity by looking at the life of one of the women in the Bible. The story of Esther gives us many things to ponder as we consider who we are. You can find her story in the Old Testament, in the book that bears her name. I encourage you to take the time to read the whole story, but here is a quick summary:

Esther lived around 500 BC. She was a Jew, but not born in Israel. The Jews had been defeated and taken in captivity by the Babylonians decades earlier. Although Babylon had since been defeated by a Persian king who had allowed the Jews to return to Israel, many Jews remained in exile, including Esther's parents. They died while she was young, and her older cousin Mordecai took her in and raised her as his own in the Persian city of Susa.

Xerxes, the king of the Persian Empire, had deposed his queen for refusing his command to make a grand entrance at his banquet so he could parade her and flaunt her beauty before his drunken friends. He was wanting a new queen, so he appointed commissioners all over his kingdom to find the most beautiful young women (probably girls in their early teens) and bring them to his harem. After months of beauty treatments, each woman would be taken to the king for a one-night stand, then returned to the harem in the morning. After "auditioning" all the women, Xerxes would choose the one who pleased him most to be his queen. The others would remain in the harem, probably for the rest of their lives.

Of all the beautiful girls, Esther was chosen to be queen. At Mordecai's instruction, she had not revealed she was Jewish. So, Esther, a Jewish exile, moved into the palace of the king of Persia. Mordecai checked on her periodically, standing at the king's gate to catch a glimpse of her. He was, at least occasionally, able to talk to her or get a message to her.

Later, King Xerxes elevated one of his nobles named Haman, giving him a higher place than all the other nobles at court. All the royal officials standing at the king's gate would give Haman special honor when he walked by, but Mordecai refused to bow before him. This enraged Haman, and when he found out Mordecai was a Jew, he decided to take his revenge not just on Mordecai, but all of Mordecai's people.

Haman presented his plan to King Xerxes: "Did you know there are a bunch of people living in exile among us? They're not our people, and they don't honor our ways. They keep themselves separate and don't follow our laws. It is in your best interest to destroy them." The king agreed, not knowing his queen was one of those people! He sent an edict to the leaders throughout his kingdom, setting a date to initiate the complete annihilation of the Jews. The date was approximately eleven months out.

When Mordecai learned about the plan, he tore his clothes and went out into the city of Susa, wailing loudly and bitterly. Esther did not yet know of the plan. When her servants came and told her about the state of her cousin, she sent one of her attendants to go find out what was wrong. Mordecai sent a copy of the edict back to Esther and asked her to intercede with the king on behalf of the Jews.

Esther sent word back to Mordecai that it would be dangerous for her to approach the king. No one, not even the queen, could approach the king without being summoned. And the king had not asked for her for thirty days as it was! Anyone who tried to gain access to the king on their own initiative would be put to death unless the king extended his gold scepter to them.

Mordecai responded to Esther:

> *"Do not think that because you are in the king's house you alone of all the Jews will escape. For if you remain silent at this time, relief and deliverance for the Jews will arise from another place, but you and your father's family will perish. And who knows but that you have come to your royal position for such a time as this?"*
>
> (Esther 4:13-14)

Esther asked Mordecai to gather the Jews in Susa to fast and pray for three days, after which she agreed to go to the king. "If I perish, I perish," she said bravely.

Fortunately, Xerxes extended his scepter to her. Esther was able to intervene on behalf of her people, and the story eventually ends with the Jews not only being spared, but being allowed to assemble, protect themselves, and plunder their enemies. It was a miraculous turnaround of events. Jews still commemorate this with the annual celebration of Purim.

A Heart Like Esther's

There is much in this story to contemplate as we consider the influences on Esther's heart. Let's allow our hearts to experience Esther's life for a few minutes. She was born in exile, growing up as an alien. Even at a young age, it would have been apparent to her that her people were different, keeping themselves separate from the citizens of Susa and following different customs. They were outcasts.

And then, while she was still young, both parents died. Now she was an orphan, taken in to grow up in the house of an older cousin. And, she was female, living in a time and place where girls were second-class citizens, with practically no rights or opportunities. Alien, orphan, female: Esther was at the bottom of the pecking order. There was nothing in her life to speak hope or value to her.

As Esther matured, she was notably beautiful, at least according to the values in the culture she grew up in. When the king sent his men out to all corners of his realm to gather the most beautiful young ladies, Esther was among the chosen. (Would you value your good looks under those circumstances?) Removed from her home, removed from her own people, Esther essentially became the property of the king. She became a contestant in a beauty contest where the audition meant a night in bed with the king. Many months were spent preparing her for this one event, with no guaranteed outcome. The entire focus was on outer beauty. Win or lose, Esther would remain a part of the king's harem. No chance to return to life with her people and have a family among them.

And then Esther became queen! Her status changed instantly. She was elevated to a position far above any of her fellow Jews. She suddenly had status, abundant provision, beautiful clothes, and people to wait on her. But she was not free to reveal her Jewish identity. She was not free to visit her childhood home. She was not free to see or discuss things with the king who had made her queen. She lived under the iron hand of Xerxes, the despot who had ousted his previous wife (See Esther 1:10-19).

About five years later—when she was perhaps in her early twenties– Esther found herself in the middle of a horrific ethnic battle. To intervene on behalf of the Jews meant risking her own life. To choose inaction meant the certain annihilation of her people.

Esther had a monumental decision to make. For most of her life, she had had few choices. She didn't choose to be Jewish, an orphan, or a female. She hadn't chosen to live in exile, to be beautiful, or to be queen of the largest kingdom in the world. Those things were thrust upon her. Now the man who had been a father to her was telling her about her king's plans for the Jews . . . and asking her to risk her life.

The Bible doesn't give us any insight into Esther's heart up to this point. We can only imagine the kinds of pain her heart had carried into her new position: fear, abandonment, grief, inferiority, self-pity, anger, self-doubt, regret, confusion, envy, and hopelessness, to name a few. And what about those other feelings that may have come into her heart when she became queen? Relief, comfort, self-satisfaction, pride?

And now? The comfort and relief she might have felt at becoming queen could have easily turned into regret: *If only I hadn't been so beautiful. If only he hadn't picked me! Isn't there someone else who could do this for Mordecai?*

Or she could have shielded herself from reality by denying the truth: *Things can't be that bad. Mordecai must be exaggerating. The king would never just annihilate all of us. Maybe just a few, but not many. Not me.*

This is all conjecture, but however Esther's heart was tormented and conflicted, we know what she clung to in the end. She chose to honor Mordecai and his request. She chose to rely on the God to whom Mordecai had probably introduced her as a child. She chose to be vulnerable to her fellow Jews by asking them to fast and pray. She chose selflessness, hope, and faith. Because of Esther's heart's posture, a nation was saved.

What We Can Learn

Esther's story exemplifies important truths for our hearts to grasp. Our circumstances, trials, backgrounds, opportunities, injustices, and heart wounds may be different from Esther's. But we all have circumstances, trials, backgrounds, opportunities, injustices, and wounded hearts! Not one of us has lived a generic life.

Dear friends, we must not let *any* of those things determine how we see our identities or purposes. Has your heart taken on the identity of an orphan, an outcast, insignificant, powerless, useless? Do you feel like your life has no impact? Have you disqualified yourself from making any difference in this world? Esther certainly could have felt like that as a young woman. And so could most of us.

There was nothing in Esther's life or circumstances that set her apart from the rest of the world. On her own, she was powerless to make an impact. She did not have any resources for promoting herself or changing her world. She had no path to influence or power. Her identity looked insignificant.

But *true* identity is not defined by position or influence or worldly resources! Identity is defined by the Creator. The past, the present, and the future are all in His hands. Esther's life was governed by God's plans for her, His people, and the world. Her significance originated in God's heart and was fulfilled by His power. Much of it was completely out of her control. The only choice she really had in the whole process was whether to say yes or no to Mordecai's request. Ultimately, the choice was whether to trust God or not. She chose to pray, and to put her life in God's hands. The rest, as they say, is history. In Esther's case, it is history that was recorded thousands of years ago, for the benefit of you and me today.

Chapter 11 Reflection

1. How would you have described your identity before reading this chapter?

_____

_____

_____

2. What are the life experiences that have informed your heart about your identity?

_____

_____

_____

3. Can you look back and see times where your sense of identity has changed because your circumstances have changed?

_____

_____

_____

4. Are you beginning to embrace the possibility of a new identity?

_____

_____

_____

Chapter 12

Or the Heart of a Grasshopper?

One summer evening when I was fourteen, my dad confided in me that he was going to divorce my mom and marry someone else. I don't remember having a particularly emotional reaction. I don't remember saying anything. As I've said, my heart was already shut down. But I do remember leaving the house and walking a couple blocks to the local elementary school. Along one edge of the schoolyard was a chain-link fence with a row of bushes in front of it. I climbed through the bushes and sat down in the dirt, leaning back against the fence.

There is probably some psychological term for this kind of weird behavior. I cannot think up one reason why I might have done that. All I know is that I was completely hidden and completely alone. I do remember wishing someone would come and get me, but I didn't know who it might be. The world was very big and very confusing. And I felt very, very small.

With that in mind, let's take a brief look at another incident about identity—one that didn't turn out so well. This is another story about the Jews, God's chosen people.

Feeling Like a Grasshopper

God had intervened in all His power and glory, delivering the Israelites from four hundred years of slavery under the Egyptians. He had confirmed His love and plans for them over and over by parting the Red Sea, providing water from rocks, and providing fresh food for them to gather every morning. When they complained that they wanted meat, enough quail were blown in overnight to cover their camp three feet deep! Surely, Israel would grasp their identity as the chosen people of the God who was making a way for them. Right?

When the people reached the border of the Promised Land, Moses sent scouts to check out the land. Sure enough, it was everything the Lord had promised, "flowing with milk and honey"—an idiom proclaiming it prosperous, fertile, and altogether awesome. They brought back a single cluster of grapes so large it took two people to carry! But the scouts noticed something else as well:

> *"We can't attack those people; they are stronger than we are. . ..*
> *The land we explored devours those living in it. All the people*
> *we saw there are of great size. We saw the Nephilim there (the*
> *descendants of Anak come from the Nephilim). We seemed like*
> *grasshoppers in our own eyes, and we looked the same to them."*
> *(Numbers 13:31–33)*

They saw gigantic men. And their hearts melted. They allowed their circumstances (in this case, the presence of warriors much bigger than they) to dictate their view of themselves ("we seemed like grasshoppers in our own eyes"). In the end, God's people bought into this diminished view of their identity and said no to the opportunity before them. Instead of moving forward and taking hold of the land God had promised them, they had to wander in the desert for forty years.

The story of David and Goliath deals with a similar prospect. The entire army of Israel was intimidated by the presence of one man, Goliath. Rather than looking to the omnipotent God who called them His own, the Israelites were fixated on his remarkable nine-foot stature and the weight of his shiny armor. They looked like grasshoppers in their own eyes, and it paralyzed them.

Goliath taunted the army of Israel for days, unopposed! It took a shepherd boy, with a heart that found its strength and identity in God, to intervene. David had a few stones in his pouch, but they were empowered by the favor and resources of God. There was no contest.

Have you ever felt like a grasshopper in overwhelming circumstances? Has your heart been tempted to assume the identity of hopeless inferiority? Have you seen yourself as an insignificant, powerless insect?

If we look at the stories of significant women in the Bible, it is apparent that not one of us is disqualified from being "significant" based on our backstory. Biblical women ran the gamut from royalty to commoner, rich to poor, country folk to city folk. The lineage of Jesus includes a prostitute (Rahab) and two women who were not Jewish (Rahab and Ruth)!

I use women of the Bible as examples because we have access to their stories. But I want to make another important point: significance is not determined by fame or worldly recognition. We do not have access to the stories of the millions and millions of women who have impacted individuals, families, cities, and civilizations throughout the history of the world. Not one woman is insignificant.

Has your heart taken on an identity inferior to what is true about you? Your significance is dictated by the fact that you were created by a God who loves you, knows you, died for you, will never leave you, and has placed you right where you are for His purposes. Esther's impact on the world was the result of lots of circumstances she had no control over. But when she had an opportunity to choose, she took hold of Mordecai's words: "Who knows but that you have come to your royal position for such a time as this?"(Esther 4:14). Her heart embraced her identity, and she placed her life in God's hands.

No matter our circumstances, we will each have moments of decision that will shape our lives and the lives of others. These decisions will ultimately flow from our *inner fountains of passion, thought, and purpose.* What does your heart trust? What does your heart fear? Whom does your heart believe *you* to be?

Your reality is the same as Esther's. *You have come to your royal position for such a time as this.*

Am I exaggerating to make a point? Absolutely not. "Royal position" suggests being in relationship with the one who is in power. It means you have their ear and their favor. It means having access to their resources. And that is our position as believers. Our King is not just an earthly king; He is Lord of heaven and earth. He is King over every other king, and Lord over every other lord. All other rulers bow to Him. He bows to none. And He has adopted *us* as His children. He has made us heirs to His kingdom. We can come to the throne room whenever we want, and his gold scepter is always extended to us. "Royal" is part of our identity!

Living Like the Royalty You Are

Wherever you go and whatever you do, you carry the presence of Jesus and His limitless resources. You carry them into a fallen world, just as Esther did. Her "royal identity," which God had placed in her from the beginning, did not protect her from the evils and dangers of her world. God never promises to protect the vital people in his plan from danger. But He does promise to be with us in all of it and to work it all for good.

In God's economy, nothing is wasted. He does not allow us to experience hardship without purpose. The Enemy cannot sneak into our lives with problems that will hinder God's purposes. God promises that *all things* work together for our good. God restricts Satan's influence in our lives to those things which will make us more like Jesus and set the stage for His good work. Everything we care about and all we are called to are safely in God's control. His plan is perfect. God's goodness for us will only be hindered if we allow those hardships to identify us, take away our hope, and blind us to what He is doing. His plan for His people will still be accomplished if we reject His truth about us, but we will miss the opportunity to be a part of it. As Mordecai said earlier, "If you remain silent at this time, relief and deliverance for the Jews will arise from another place."

When we turn back to God's truth about our hearts, the promise is waiting for us, and we are restored to our purpose. This work of grace doesn't make sense to our finite minds. If we are such a vital part of God's plan, how can we drop the ball without wrecking the plan? How can the plan go on without our vital role? And if the plan moves forward without us and then we get back in the game, how can it turn out perfectly? This is one of those places where God's promises must take hold of our hearts, even when our minds cannot understand.

Truth comes from an infinite place where seemingly contradictory things fit together perfectly. My *inner fountain of passion, thought, and purpose* must reach beyond what is rational and take hold of what is true about me. Just as Esther's mind could not possibly grasp the immensity of God's plans for her, our minds cannot comprehend the depths of our identities and purposes . . . or God's fierceness in defending His calling on our lives.

If the Enemy had his way, we would experience absolute devastation and destruction without any hope that it would be redeemed and turned to good. But the truth is that God was sovereign over every detail of Esther's life. And He is sovereign over our lives as well.

Royal position is part of your identity. You were created for this time and place. Like everyone, there are aspects of your life you did not choose. But you can choose how to carry your heart amid those circumstances.

Are you experiencing identity theft? In the natural world, our finances, reputation, and physical security can be threatened by criminals who hack into computer systems and obtain information to take advantage of. If your bank informs you someone has stolen your identity, it would be prudent to believe them and take necessary defensive action! However, when you are bombarded with lies about your identity—and these can come in your thoughts as well as from those around you—do *not* believe them! Do not believe any voices telling you that you've caused irreparable damage, that the obstacles in your life are too big, that too much has gone wrong, that God doesn't care. There is necessary action for you to take here. Engage your *passions, thoughts, and purposes* in declaring what is true about your identity. Face the Enemy straight on and remind yourself in no uncertain terms that he is a liar! Take the offensive and run toward the Enemy like David did Goliath, with big, heavy golden nuggets of truth in your sling! Here are some nuggets to keep in your pouch:

> *If anyone is in Christ, this person is a new creation: the old things passed away; behold, new things have come.*
>
> *(2 Corinthians 5:17, NASB)*

> *"I no longer call you servants, because a servant does not know his master's business. Instead, I have called you friends, for everything that I learned from my Father I have made known to you. You did not choose me, but I chose you and appointed you so that you might go and bear fruit—fruit that will last—and so that whatever you ask in my name the Father will give you."*
>
> *(John 15:15-16)*

> *See what great love the Father has lavished on us, that we should be called children of God! And that is what we are! The reason the world does not know us is that it did not know him.*
>
> *(1 John 3:1)*

Yet to all who did receive him, to those who believed in his name, he gave the right to become children of God—children born not of natural descent, nor of human decision or a husband's will, but born of God.

(John 1:12-13)

Therefore, there is now no condemnation for those who are in Christ Jesus.

(Romans 8:1)

In all these things we are more than conquerors through him who loved us. For I am convinced that neither death nor life, neither angels nor demons, neither the present nor the future, nor any powers, neither height nor depth, nor anything else in all creation, will be able to separate us from the love of God that is in Christ Jesus our Lord.

(Romans 8: 37-39)

Before I formed you in the womb I knew you, before you were born I set you apart.

(Jeremiah 1:5)

You are a chosen people, a royal priesthood, a holy nation, God's special possession, that you may declare the praises of him who called you out of darkness into his wonderful light.

(1 Peter 2:9)

Your identity is secure in the heart of your Father. If you look to anything else for your identity, you will become a slave to that thing. Your *inner fountain of passion, thought, and purpose* will elevate that thing above God, and it will ensnare you.

Your story may not become well known. You may not make it into the history books. Your name may not stand out in your family tree. Your funeral may not be attended by huge crowds. But none of those things determine your identity, your significance, or your impact. Do not let the values of this world, your circumstances, or your weaknesses tell your heart how important you are. Yours is the heart of a queen, come to its royal position for such a time as this. God's purposes in this world *will* prevail, and you are part of those purposes. You are God's chosen woman, and this is your appointed time.

Chapter 12 Reflection

1. In what areas have you felt like a grasshopper? Can you identify lies that you have believed about your identity?

_____

_____

_____

_____

_____

2. In what ways is your heart able to believe and act on its royal position?

_____

_____

_____

_____

3. In what ways do you question or reject the concept of royal position?

_____

_____

_____

_____

Part Five:
A Handbook for Our Hearts

Chapter 13

Forgiveness

O ur bodies have an amazing ability to heal. And science is increasingly able to help us deal with wounds. Stitch up a wound, and off you go. A broken bone can be set and immobilized—stay off that foot, keep that arm in a sling, and within a few weeks you will be good to go. A bruise is just a bruise; don't bang it again for a while, and soon you won't be able to remember where it was. And for the worst of cases, many broken body parts can now be replaced!

Hearts—our *inner fountains of passion, thought, and purpose*—are more complex. For one thing, they're eternal, extending far beyond what science will ever discover. Science has not provided us with x-rays, surgical techniques, or replacement parts for a wounded heart. A broken heart is difficult to assess. Wounds that look minor can actually be very deep.

There is one similarity between hearts and bodies: wounds that are not properly treated can fester. Infection does its deadly work, unseen on the surface. Much of the horror we see around us is the explosive result of heart wounds that have festered for years.

Physically, most of us in the Western world are relatively safe today. We generally do not have to endanger life or limb to live a normal life. There will be cuts and scrapes along the way, but most of us have access to help when our bodies need it.

The same is not true for our hearts. Every morning, our hearts wake up to people and situations that will challenge them. Disappointments, betrayals, misunderstandings . . . there is no way to avoid them. Our hearts were made for relationship, and relationship is *always* messy! Imperfect hearts collide with imperfect hearts, and those hearts injure each other.

Our hearts' journey to wholeness requires the healing and restoration of past wounds, but we must also attend to our hearts' responses to today's potential perils. The Bible gives us wisdom on how to avoid many dangers, and we will visit many aspects of that wisdom in this part of the book. But we can only control our *own* decisions. The decisions and actions of those around us have the potential to jab at our hearts and cause injury.

It seems the only way to protect our hearts might be to cloister ourselves away, alone. If there is no one around to mess with our hearts, they should be safe, right? No. Hearts are made for relationship. Protecting our hearts by keeping them away from people would be like shunning all food to avoid poisoning our bodies. A completely isolated heart will eventually shrivel up and die. Isolation brings loneliness, despair, and emotional instability. Isolation is so devastating, it is considered one of the harshest punishments: solitary confinement!

Help and Healing for the Wounded Heart

So, how can we deal with those hidden and not-so-hidden wounds we've carried for so long?

How can our hearts navigate life without taking on each new wound of neglect, disappointment, misunderstanding, and various wrongs and abuses? Every interaction that devalues us in some way is an injustice. Big or little, devastating or even comical, injustices threaten our hearts in two ways. First of all, there is the real pain of not being valued and cared for. It hurts, period. And *then*, secondly, our hearts are in a precarious position where their responses to that injustice may bring themselves further wounding.

For the pain, I know of only one remedy: get comfort. Let the One who will never leave you, forsake you, or betray you come alongside you. I addressed comfort in detail in Chapter 3, but I want to emphasize it again here. Do not miss an opportunity to let God hold your heart in its grieving. Don't let that pain crawl to a corner of your heart and fester!

But then—and this is important—quickly surrender that pain to Him. If you're having trouble letting go of it, ask Him for help. It may take time, but He is *faithful*. He does not ignore or downplay our pain. But He will not indulge it. Jesus has ushered new life into the world, and He invites us to give Him the past and move forward. God tells us:

> *Forget the former things; do not dwell on the past. See, I am doing a new thing! Now it springs up; do you not perceive it? I am making a way in the wilderness and streams in the wasteland.*
>
> *(Isaiah 43:18-19)*

Many of us have embraced our pain and allowed it to become a part of our worldview and identity. It is so easy to take on the identity of a victim, of a weak and defenseless woman. The Enemy is exceedingly creative in using injustices against us in this way. But let's not be women who find our identities in our pain. We must let injustices turn our hearts to the God of all comfort, and then take His hand and pursue *new* lives and *new* identities in Him.

A crucial next step in our new life in Christ is to learn to guard our responses to injustice. Bitterness, revenge, fear, anger, hatred: these are natural responses. But they will hinder and suppress our hearts' proper function. They build walls in our relationships with God and others. They color our view of ourselves, others, and life. If these things are allowed to lodge themselves in our *inner fountains of passion, thought, and purpose*, they will distort how we think, feel, and act. They wrap chains around our God-given gifts and burden our hearts with weights they weren't designed to carry.

The Apostle Paul warned the believers in Ephesus about these things, telling them, "Get rid of all bitterness, rage and anger, brawling and slander, along with every form of malice" (Ephesians 4:31). Get rid of them! Throw them out! Remove them! Why? Because they injure your heart and the hearts of those around you. This instruction from Paul is for the sake of your heart.

There's just one problem here. *How?* How do we get rid of them? Can we just tell the bitterness and disappointment to go away? Can we just hold those hateful, vengeful thoughts out in the palms of our hands and blow them into the atmosphere? Not a chance. Paul goes on to tell us how to do it:

> *Get rid of all bitterness, rage and anger, brawling and slander, along with every form of malice. Be kind and compassionate to one another, forgiving each other, just as in Christ God forgave you.*
> (*Ephesians 4:31–32*)

This verse contains a vital secret about whole hearts. It gives us a tool for healing our hearts and protecting the hearts of others. "Be kind and compassionate to one another." Simple and straightforward, but oh so difficult. Difficult because those people to whom we are supposed to be kind and understanding are likely the ones who have *not* been kind and understanding to us. Paul knew it would be difficult, so he told us the secret: "forgiving each other."

Forgiveness: Your Secret Weapon

Forgiving sounds simple and straightforward. But not only is it difficult, it sometimes feels downright impossible. Paul addressed that as well. To be able to forgive, we must tap into the forgiveness Jesus extended to us: "just as in Christ God forgave you."

Let's put it together: "Be kind and compassionate to one another, forgiving each other, just as in Christ God forgave you." Paul is talking about the power of forgiveness that exists in the heart of God. Forgiveness is at the core of the nature of God, but not at all core to the fallen nature of mankind. God loosed the supernatural power of forgiveness into the world when Jesus died for us. And we tapped into that supernatural power when we received His forgiveness. The ability to forgive is part of our inheritance as those who are no longer citizens of this bitter, evil, self-centered world. We do not have to take up an offense. We have been forgiven, and that empowers us to forgive others.

Jesus is our example. He certainly had reason for bitterness, anger, and hatred! Betrayed by the very people He came to minister to, abandoned by His own disciples, and hung on a cross like a common criminal, His heart was exposed to humans at their worst. Injustice attacked Him from every side. As Isaiah states it:

> "He was despised and rejected—a man of sorrows, acquainted with deepest grief. We turned our backs on him and looked the other way. He was despised, and we did not care."
>
> (Isaiah 53:3, NLT)

His response to betrayal, abandonment, and agony? As He was hanging on the cross, He prayed, "Father, forgive them" (Luke 23:34).

Forgive. I believe this will bring the greatest challenge, and the greatest healing, to your heart. The ability to forgive may seem unreachable for those of you who have suffered horrific abuses. It's hard enough for those of us who deal with the simple injustices of being ignored or misunderstood or inconvenienced! How can we forgive?

Jesus gives us some perspective with a parable in which a servant owed his master the equivalent of millions of dollars. His master ordered the servant, his wife, his children, and all his belongings to be sold to repay the debt. The servant fell on his knees and begged for mercy, and his master forgave the debt. That same servant then went out and confronted a man who owed him a day's wages, and he had that man thrown into prison! The servant who had been forgiven millions of dollars of debt had no mercy on the man who owed him a small fraction of that (see Matthew 18:20-30).

Jesus told this parable to make a point: we owe God "millions of dollars," yet He has forgiven each of us completely. We have rejected His love, ignored His presence, disregarded His ways, and refused His lordship in more ways than we will ever know. Our sin is deeper and wider than we can begin to imagine. And Jesus took it all to the cross. He bore the weight of all of it. He *knows* the cost of forgiveness.

Compared to all He has forgiven us, we have little to forgive, even when it comes to the ones who have hurt us most. We have no right to make our offenders pay for what they have done to us. Jesus already paid for us *and* for them.

Again, God does not ignore or downplay the injustices we have experienced. He does not ask us to pretend we aren't bothered by them. He does not ask us to forgive because our pain and others' sins don't matter. He does not ask us to maintain our hearts in some lofty place where they are impervious to injustice. No. He asks us to walk *through* the pain and humiliation just like Jesus did. Forgiveness is how we do it. And we do not do it alone.

Jesus knows our pain, and He will take us by the hand. He has holy, eternal purposes for our hearts, and this walk with Him strengthens our hearts and prepares them for eternity. Our hearts become like His through this process.

For some of you, this process might have to begin by actually acknowledging that an injustice has been done to you. The Enemy wants us to rationalize that what happened really doesn't matter. Or even worse, that we only have received what we deserved. Our abusers are happy to reinforce those lies: "You made me do it!" "How stupid can you be?" "You will never change!"

Let me emphasize . . . those are *lies*! Your Father has some truth for you: your value and identity come from Him. It is not something you earn, nor something you can lose by how you act or how you are treated.

Let's park here a minute and get God's perspective. In messy relationships, where people are hurting each other and being hurt, *all* the people involved are precious to God. God is looking at your situation and caring deeply about you *and* the other person. He loves you both. He has glorious plans for both of you. And, in His love and wisdom, He has instructions for both of you. God's instructions are being ignored by the one who is hurting you. But God asks you to let Him be the one who defends you. God does not want your heart to take on the burden of making someone else pay.

Forgiveness is an act of faith. Only God has the wisdom to defend you, bring justice, and redeem every person who can be redeemed. Will you leave vengeance in His hands, allowing Him to determine the fate of those who have wronged you? Is it okay for Him to extend the same grace to them that He has extended to you? Will you trust His *eternal* justice? He has promised to repay, but that likely won't happen according to your perspective or your timeline:

> *Do not take revenge, my dear friends, but leave room for God's wrath, for it is written: "It is mine to avenge; I will repay," says the Lord. On the contrary: "If your Enemy is hungry, feed him; if he is thirsty, give him something to drink. In doing this, you*

will heap burning coals on his head." Do not be overcome by
evil, but overcome evil with good.

(Romans 12:19-21)

This passage sheds some light on the power of forgiveness. Hanging on to anger and bitterness puts us in danger of being overcome by evil. Forgiveness actually looses good that overcomes evil, light that overcomes darkness. Scripture often reminds us vengeance belongs to God:

For we know him who said, "Vengeance is mine; I will repay."
And again, "The Lord will judge his people." It is a fearful thing
to fall into the hands of the living God.

(Hebrews 10:31–31, ESV)

When we let go of our desire for revenge, we are placing the other person into the hands of our Father! And will our Father not defend us appropriately?

What Forgiveness Looks Like

I think we tend to underestimate the anger of our loving Father toward those who harm us. He does not turn a blind eye or gloss over the injustices we have experienced. His hands are a dreadful place for the one who has harmed His daughter. Forgiveness does not mean letting abusers off the hook; it means letting God choose how and when to repay.

What does forgiveness look like? Forgiveness says, "I let go of the right to make you suffer for what you did to me. You do not owe me anything, and I do not count anything against you." Forgiveness frees your heart from a burden it was never meant to carry.

In every situation, forgiveness is first a choice. That seems doable. Our inner fountains of *thought* can take God at His word and inform our *purposes* that we are going to forgive. . .but those *passions* are not so easily influenced, are they?

The famous "love chapter" in the Bible, 1 Corinthians 13, says, "Love keeps no record of wrongs" (1 Corinthians 13:5). But we *do* keep a record, and we review it often. It's on our Favorites playlist, so one click can quickly bring it up. We shuffle it. We replay it. We are so far from being able to love the way Jesus does! Forgiveness is part of that love, but our hearts prefer to keep the record of injustices and play it often. Our *passion* has a lot of fuel for the fire of unforgiveness.

We need supernatural help. We can go to the One who understands exactly what we're going through and ask Him for help. I am reminded of the father whose son was seized by a spirit that made him unable to speak. The father asked Jesus to heal his son, but his faith was weak. He exclaimed, "I do believe; help me overcome my unbelief" (Mark 9:24). Similarly, our hearts cry out, "I do forgive! Help me overcome my unforgiveness!" We will find in God an understanding and powerful Helper.

Jesus said forgiveness is something we must persist in:

> *Then Peter came to Jesus and asked, "Lord, how many times shall I forgive my brother or sister who sins against me? Up to seven times?" Jesus answered, "I tell you, not seven times, but seventy-seven times."*
>
> *(Matthew 18:21-22)*

In this fallen world, there will always be people throwing darts and daggers at our hearts by their words and actions. We each have that person who does it over and over. And everywhere we will encounter those who, whether meaning to or not, will fling a careless arrow in our direction. There are missiles flying all over the place. And we are asked to live with a continuous attitude of forgiveness. We *can* do it by first choosing, then trusting, then rejoicing and growing as we find He is indeed making us more like Jesus. Forgiveness has been loosed in this world, and we are part of an army of forgiven people who can overcome the stranglehold bitterness and rage have on the earth.

There is another aspect of forgiveness that is essential to whole hearts, and that is our ability to *receive* forgiveness. Many of us keep a playlist of our own mistakes, queued up right with that playlist of others' offenses against us. Our hearts are visited by shame, regret, and condemnation, all of which are crippling.

Dear friends, we *have* blown it, over and over and over. Those self-willed things we have done even though we knew better, those hurtful words or actions birthed in ignorance or misunderstanding, those inno-cent or reckless mistakes, those words we engineered to land like daggers in someone's heart, those careless words we want to take back the minute they leave our mouths . . . we all have a long history of these things. No device has enough storage for this playlist!

The Holy Spirit protects our hearts by making us uncomfortable with our sin. The Bible calls this godly sorrow, and it has a healthy, redemp-tive purpose: "Godly sorrow brings repentance that leads to salvation and leaves no regret, but worldly sorrow brings death" (2 Corinthians 7:10).

God does not intend for us to entertain shame, regret, or condem-nation—these leave our hearts wallowing in what is wrong with us. They rob us of the life God intends for us. But God *does* intend for us to move away from our sin. Repentance acknowledges before God that we are guilty, and expresses our willingness and desire to be changed. It looses the power of forgiveness in our own hearts, opening the door for cleans-ing and healing:

> *If we claim to be without sin, we deceive ourselves and the truth
> is not in us. If we confess our sins, he is faithful and just and
> will forgive us our sins and purify us from all unrighteousness.*
> *(1 John 1:8-9)*

Here's one more thought that may haunt us: "I don't deserve to be free of regret." Well, actually, that is true. But nothing in this book is about what we *deserve*. It's all about joyfully and confidently taking hold of everything Jesus freely offers us. This is the life of faith that pleases God. It does *not* please God for us to refuse anything He has provided! Jesus has purchased for us the right to leave our sin *along with regret* at the foot of the cross: "There is therefore now no condemnation for those who are in Christ Jesus" (Romans 8:1, ESV).

With the help of the Holy Spirit, we can discern between the Lord's whispers which bring godly sorrow, and the condemning voices that seek to destroy. We can steward our hearts by extending forgiveness to others when they assault us and by receiving forgiveness when we have blown it. As we mature in forgiveness, our broken hearts will become more like the whole heart of Jesus.

Chapter 13 Reflection

1. Are there things from your past that your heart has taken on as part of your identity? (e.g., betrayal, abuse, poverty, rejection, insignificance, etc.)

_____

_____

_____

_____

_____

2. What have the important people in your life said to you that have become part of your identity?

_____

_____

_____

_____

_____

3. Are you beginning to see that your identity is not tied to the things in those first two questions?

_____

_____

_____

_____

_____

4. Where have you held on to unforgiveness?

_____

_____

_____

_____

_____

_____

_____

5. Where has it been difficult for you to receive God's forgiveness?

_____

_____

_____

_____

_____

_____

_____

Chapter 14

Your Body

I don't know one woman who is just delighted with her body. At some point in our lives, perhaps without articulating it, most of us come to the realization that we are trapped in bodies we don't like very much.

I look back and see it started for me in my early teens. That was when I became aware of girls being noticed for their appearance. Boys admired bodies. Other girls admired good looks. I was a loser on both counts.

I was a late bloomer. I had bony legs and a scrawny body. My acne was horrible. Other girls had an innate sense of what the "in" fashions were; I always felt a step or two behind. I had to wear glasses. My hair, though blond, was thin and wouldn't grow long. There was an inner conflict between my desire to wear the boys' clothes I liked (which the school didn't allow anyway), and my desire to be admired for my looks. I never was at peace with my body.

Many in my generation experienced some degree of this in our early teens. But the current incessant bombardment of the media assaults even our little girls with reasons to bemoan their looks. Body angst is common among females of all ages.

Why, oh why, do our hearts have to put up with bodies anyway? In His wisdom, God has crafted this glorious planet as the environment where our hearts mature. Our relationship with Him is forged here where we encounter choices and trials that challenge our hearts and require us to lean on Him. And to experience life on Earth, we need bodies.

Scripture is clear that the Lord has revealed Himself in creation. One of the purposes of a body, then, is to experience Him in creation. We need our senses to inform our hearts of the wonder—the sights, the smells, the immensity, the minute detail, the beauty, the glory—of God's creation:

> *The heavens declare the glory of God; the skies proclaim the work of his hands.*
>
> *(Psalm 19:1)*

> *Lift up your eyes and look to the heavens: Who created all these? He who brings out the starry host one by one and calls forth each of them by name. Because of his great power and mighty strength, not one of them is missing.*
>
> *(Isaiah 40:26)*

> *For since the creation of the world God's invisible qualities— his eternal power and divine nature—have been clearly seen, being understood from what has been made, so that people are without excuse.*
>
> *(Romans 1:20)*

Our bodies also experience God's provision and comfort. King David responds to God's provision as he instructs his soul:

Praise the LORD, *my soul, and forget not all his benefits—who forgives all your sins and heals all your diseases, who redeems your life from the pit and crowns you with love and compassion, who satisfies your desires with good things so that your youth is renewed like the eagle's.*

(Psalm 103:2–5)

This is the whole heart in action: our thoughts instruct our passions and purposes to worship as our bodies experience God in creation.

Our bodies also experience the depravity of Satan's dominion in this world: hunger, murder, rape, famine, injustice, poverty, illness, death. These physical experiences ravage our hearts, but they also give us the opportunity to trust God and experience His victorious goodness in the context of trials. The magnitude of God's redemptive power in this world is demonstrated as we bring Him into our physical struggles.

Our bodies are essential in carrying out many of the activities of the heart. It is our bodies which experience much of the give and take of relationship. We need bodies in order to love as God calls us to love: "Love is patient, love is kind" (1 Corinthians 13:4). Staying up all night to comfort a sick child, not lashing out at someone who just cut in front of you, preparing a meal for everyone when you're exhausted and don't even want to eat . . . these acts of love and kindness require our hearts to engage our bodies as well.

God is not ignorant of the problems of the physical body. Jesus became flesh! He experienced the joys and pains of the physical world. He enjoyed the taste of good wine at a wedding, and the physical closeness of a beloved friend leaning on his breast. He experienced the frustrations of crowds constantly invading his space, and the physical pain of nails driven into his hands and feet. When we come to Him with our weaknesses, He understands because He knows firsthand what it's like to live in a human body.

Learning to Love Your Body

The Bible tells us that God oversees the development of each of us in our mother's womb:

> *For you created my inmost being; you knit me together in my mother's womb. I praise you because I am fearfully and wonderfully made; your works are wonderful, I know that full well.*
>
> *(Psalm 139:13–14)*

The human body should evoke reverence and awe. The world presumes to judge this handiwork of God with a ranking system that has nothing to do with God's priorities or purposes. Shall we go to God, shoving our bodies in His face, and ask Him why He made us this way? Shall we show Him a picture of someone the world calls beautiful and ask why He couldn't have fashioned us after them? Should we impose the distorted judgments of our peers on what He has created? Most of us would be quick to say no, but an honest examination may reveal that some of our judgments and desires line up with the world's. It is essential that we tear our hearts away from this system, being careful not to judge ourselves or others by its demonic inspiration.

I find myself having to engage in this battle over and over. I no longer have the angst of my early teen years, but I do sometimes wish my body were different in one way or another. I have found that a good—but sometimes difficult—beginning is thanksgiving. With a tentative voice, I begin, "Thank you, Father, for giving me this body. Thank you for knitting it together especially for me. Help me to embrace it, love it, and care for it." Do not be afraid to acknowledge your need for His help to accept your body! God honors our desires to have His perspective, and He knows we need His help.

With all that is wrong in our lives and the world, it is tempting to think our body image issues are too small to bother God with. But these are also heart issues! Paul instructed us: "In everything give thanks; for this is God's will for you in Christ Jesus" (1 Thessalonians 5:18, NASB). If we are struggling to give thanks for something, it is a legitimate call to prayer! Our tendency to be unhappy with something God knit together for us is not trivial. Every time we engage in the battle to get God's perspective on this issue, our hearts mature. We need God to extend His mercy to these hearts that presume to judge His work, and we need His grace to help us gain a new perspective. He promises us both grace and mercy: "Let us then approach God's throne of grace with confidence, so that we may receive mercy and find grace to help us in our time of need" (Hebrews 4:16).

Our hearts all experience the struggles of maintaining not only healthy perspectives, but also healthy habits for our bodies. For most of us, "struggles" is not a strong enough word. "Battles"? "Wars"? For many, it is daily open combat!

Our bodies were made to enjoy all of God's creation, turning our hearts in worship and thanksgiving to our Father. But healthy enjoyment has been distorted by the effects of The Fall. The Enemy loves to move in and twist God's purposes, turning blessings into idols, goodness into chains. It is easy for physical pleasures to become sources of frustration and confusion! Too much to eat, not enough to eat. A preoccupation with exercise, a refusal to get off the couch. Inappropriate sexual activity (more about that in the next chapter), or the abuse of various substances. These can become life-wrecking habits.

Many of these habits are not simply an overindulgence in physical pleasure; the Enemy has tricked us into utilizing these to distract us from our wounded hearts. He loves to see us replace one misery with another. We may feel better for a while, but we are still trapped in brokenness. Our bodies were made for experiencing the goodness of God, not to bring our wounded hearts into more bondage.

The medical community has given names to some of these imbalances and is working to help us overcome them. And I do not want to discourage partnering with the medical community when it comes to destructive habits and addictions. But I want to put first things first. These issues are not fundamentally physical. These are issues of broken hearts that have not embraced their bodies as vessels for the Father's good plans. Our bodies are not tools for medicating broken hearts. A heart that believes lies about the body it resides in will exert its influence and sabotage even the best medical efforts to care for itself. By God's grace, our hearts *and* our bodies can be healed.

Another important aspect of this (or any other issue of the heart): avoid tackling this alone. God did not give your heart the strength to stand by itself. Relationship and community are central to *all* our life and growth. You should have people who know you well enough to pray specifically for your struggles. Surround yourself with people who will love you through your failures and speak the truth when you need to hear it. And the truth you need to hear most often is that God is *for* you, and by His grace you *will* be victorious! One of the supreme advantages of community is that it allows people to walk with you and believe God for you when your own faith is weak.

We'll talk more about community in Chapter 19, but let's look at an example from the book of Exodus. Moses had led the Israelites out of Egypt, and the Amalekite army attacked them on their way to the Promised Land. Moses told Joshua to choose some men and go to battle against the Amalekites.

> *The Amalekites came and attacked the Israelites at Rephidim. Moses said to Joshua, "Choose some of our men and go out to fight the Amalekites. Tomorrow I will stand on top of the hill with the staff of God in my hands." So Joshua fought the Amalekites as Moses had ordered, and Moses, Aaron and Hur went to the top of the hill. As long as Moses held up his hands, the Israelites were winning, but whenever he lowered his hands,*

*the Amalekites were winning. When Moses' hands grew tired,
they took a stone and put it under him and he sat on it. Aaron
and Hur held his hands up—one on one side, one on the
other—so that his hands remained steady till sunset. So Joshua
overcame the Amalekite army with the sword.*

(Exodus 17:8–13)

At the beginning of the story, Joshua was instructed to go fight
the Amalekites. At the end of the story, Joshua overcame them. If
that's all we knew, we might give all the credit to Joshua. But Joshua
did not fight this battle alone! He took men into battle with him,
and he left someone behind (Moses) praying for them. Moses did not
have the strength to pray through the entire battle, so he needed help
(Aaron and Hur). This six-verse battle story includes a warrior, men
to fight with him, a man to pray for him, and physical assistants for
the one praying.

Attitudes, habits and addictions are formidable challenges to your
heart. You may not be fighting an entire Amalekite army, but your battle
is just as intense, and just as important. Do not do it alone!

And don't forget to engage your heart's companion. In this fallen
world, our bodies tend to bow before the world's fickle and deceptive
(and constantly shifting!) image of perfection, and at the altar of their
own desires. But when you receive Jesus as your Savior, He comes and
resides *in your body* in the person of the Holy Spirit. You can fight this
battle from the inside out:

*Do you not know that your bodies are temples of the Holy
Spirit,* **who is in you,** *whom you have received from God? You
are not your own; you were bought at a price. Therefore honor
God with your bodies.*

(1 Corinthians 6:19-20, emphasis mine)

God will truly be honored as you love and care for the body He gave you. Jesus is the final victor in all your battles against the Deceiver and Accuser, and you can take up the power of His resurrection and be victorious. Your body *can* experience and enjoy the wonders and pleasures of this world without being controlled by them.

Chapter 14 Reflection

1. Are there things that you have disliked about your body? Can you identify social pressures, or things people have said, or other sources of your dissatisfaction?

_____

_____

_____

_____

2. How does your heart respond to the exhortation to thank God for your body?

_____

_____

_____

_____

3. In what areas do you feel hopeless and powerless in caring for your body? Take time to invite the Holy Spirit and reengage in the battle. As a child of God, you are empowered to move forward. Remember, it is a _journey_.

_____

_____

_____

_____

_____

Chapter 15

Sex

S ex originated in the heart of God. He created us as sexual beings. Sex is good for our bodies, and good for our hearts. It should be celebrated as evidence of God's goodness to us. But like so much of what God has given us, Satan has introduced deception and perversion that can rob us of the joy of this aspect of our being. Because of this, it is crucial that we understand and adhere to God's original design for sex.

The Bible is clear about appropriate sexual activity. Is this because God is a partypooper who wants to impose harsh limits that inhibit our enjoyment of life? No! Exactly the opposite is true: *God's instructions for sexual activity are rooted in how much He treasures our hearts.* Unwanted pregnancies and debilitating sexually transmitted diseases might be avoided, but these are not the only dangers in unrestrained sexual activity. The many threats to our hearts are deep and devastating.

God's Design for Sex

We are a people in love with freedom. Our hearts long for freedom. Our Father wants us to be free; Jesus died to set us free. But the freedom Jesus purchased for us looks nothing like the "freedom" the world is peddling to us. We live in a society that wants to cast off all restraint and do what feels good in the moment. And nowhere is this pattern more rampant than in today's sexual environment.

I realize I am swimming upstream here. Voices attacking the "archaic" suggestion that sex should be reserved for marriage thunder all around us Much mainstream rhetoric claims the moral, physical, emotional, and spiritual high ground in promoting unrestrained sexual activity.

Recently, I spent some time in the medical facility of a large military base. On each table in the waiting room and in each magazine rack were dozens of copies of a glossy twenty-four-page brochure promoting various kinds of birth control. This brochure wasn't just passing along helpful information; it was *promoting* unrestrained sexual activity. The whole medical facility had become a billboard, marketing the presumption that every man and woman would be—and should be—sexually active. If everyone could just avoid pregnancies and diseases, everything would be fine.

Ladies, this is a lie from the pit of hell.

I cannot sound the alarm loudly enough. Sex is perhaps the place where our hearts are most vulnerable. There is no such thing as "casual sex" because sex is not simply a transitory physical act. We cannot separate our hearts from our sexual activity.

Jesus said, "Therefore *what God has joined together*, let no one separate" (Matthew 19:6, emphasis mine). Sex is more than a casual joining of two bodies! Sex invokes the power of God to permanently join two people together. This joining involves their entire beings, extending beyond the moment intercourse ends and their bodies separate. God has designed us so that when we join ourselves sexually with another person, we are joining our hearts to them.

I'll say it again: Sexual union involves more than just the body. We cannot give our bodies away without giving our hearts away. When you join yourself to another, you are joining your *inner fountain of passion, thought, and purpose* with theirs. Both hearts are affected. There is no clean break for either one because God designed this intermingling to bless both hearts with a unity and complementary dependency that exists in no other earthly relationship.

Because of this, there is no safe sex outside a committed, lifetime relationship. Every time we engage in a fleeting sexual relationship, we expose our hearts to wreckage. Every time we extract ourselves from a sexual relationship, our hearts experience the ripping effects of confusion, rejection, and betrayal.

Sex is not just an activity; it is a *force*. Frankly, the vastness of the power and drive of sex is something I don't claim to comprehend. But God, in His infinite wisdom and purpose, created mankind as sexual beings. Sex is a gift from our Creator, and He understands the force He has unleashed among us. That is why He has been so specific in instructing us how to steward this gift. Used rightly, it glorifies God and blesses mankind. Used wrongly, it is destructive.

God designed sex to be powerful. It is the driving force behind the most important and influential interpersonal relationship on Earth: the complete giving of oneself to another in marriage. Marriage is central to family, and family is central to healthy hearts and healthy societies.

Sex is not intended to be separate from marriage. Sex is about committed, unbroken, lifelong relationship and family. Satan is aggressively opposed to these things because they bear the image of God. The Enemy has worked patiently over time, twisting and shaping the sexual fabric of the planet to distort it in any way he can. The distortion has taken different shapes over the centuries, but the effect is the same: hearts and lives have been severely compromised.

Keeping sex within its intended boundaries saves us much heartache. Consider childbearing for example. Imagine no pregnancies outside marriage. All children would be born to a mother and father who were married to each other. The traumatic effects of extramarital pregnancies on the hearts of men, women, mothers, fathers, families, and children cannot be underestimated. God's clear, intentional instructions for sex are rooted in His love for us. When His boundaries are violated, everything breaks down.

Sex is an area where we must diligently protect our hearts. Shelter your heart behind the truth and ask God to help you proceed in purity and wisdom. A woman considering sexual activity is standing on the edge of a precipice. The only safe move forward is to wait for marriage. Jumping off outside marriage exposes her heart to injury. God's instructions are the only way to build a solid bridge over the chasm.

As with our other topics, there is much to be said about the responsibility of men in these matters. When either men *or* women abuse sex, there are tragic consequences, and I don't want to minimize the experience of those who have suffered at the hands of men. Many have a twisted and painful view of sex because of how they have been treated. For those who have been violated, I pray that our Father will visit you with comfort and healing. Ask Him into your pain. Then let Him lead you into an understanding of the truth. We must each contend for genuine freedom in this area of our lives.

Your Sexuality Is a Blessing: Use It Wisely

Let's talk about how we as women can bless and be blessed by the sexual nature of humanity. I believe the sexual drive God gave mankind empowers women to be a stabilizing, unifying influence in society. Women can participate in taming this force for the joy and blessing it is intended to bring. It is not my intent to place on women the full burden or responsibility of taming sexuality, but consider this: if all women said no to all men's advances outside the covenantal relationship of marriage, we would change society's landscape! If a man had to commit himself to a woman before having sex, then more men would commit! If there were no other women who would accept his advances, he would keep coming home to his wife.

I am not reducing marriage to merely a sexual contract. The dynamics of marriage are many and complex, and I don't want to be casual about defining it (we will hear more about marriage in the next chapter). But I also want to be clear: marriage *is*, among other things, a sexual covenant! And sex is intended to be enjoyed only in the context of this commitment.

I realize this picture of perfection seems naïve in this broken world. Men can be a formidable force to deal with, and women really are victims at times, especially in some cultures. But most of us *are* in charge of our own bodies. We need not give in to our own desires or those of men. By God's grace, the truth can prevail, and we can be women who articulate and model God's intentions for sex. We can protect our own hearts and influence the hearts of others.

Men are not the only ones with a sex drive! It is generally true that sex is more often a preoccupation for men, but women have desires as well. The rules are the same for us, and for the same reasons. Sex, as a force, is intended to stabilize and bless the covenant of marriage.

One of the original commands given to Adam and Eve was to "be fruitful and multiply." Is there any other command of God that requires us to engage in such blessed activity? But the activity is blessed only within its appropriate boundaries. And "multiplying" is intended only for married couples, because it is God's intent that children be born into family.

I must add two important cautions to this picture. It is vital you guard your own heart in matters of sex, but it is also important to care for the hearts of the men around you. I will be brief, but adamant:

First, suggestive or seductive attitudes, dress, and behavior are *never* appropriate, except in the context of marriage. Be beautiful, be sporty, be creative, be wild, be cute, be comfy, be fun, be you . . .but do it in modesty and holiness. Do not tempt!

Second, sex *within* marriage should be joyfully and freely given and received. Sex is not intended to be a tool for manipulation or retribution.

Let's look at a succinct command from the Apostle Paul: "Flee from sexual immorality" (1 Corinthians 6:18). This is straightforward. We can't look to the Greek for wiggle room. The Greek word translated "flee" means to run away as fast as you can because you are not safe! This is the same word used to describe Joseph and Mary fleeing to Egypt because Herod was looking to kill Jesus (see Matthew 2:13) and Moses fleeing Egypt because Pharoah wanted to kill him (see Acts 7:29).

The Greek word translated "sexual immorality" is *porneia*, which refers to any sexual activity outside the marriage between a man and a woman. Paul's meaning couldn't be clearer: *run* from any sexual encounter outside marriage. Avoid compromising situations. Don't be there.

To echo Proverbs 4:23 again: "Above all else, guard your heart." Flee from sexual immorality! It is a loving command from a wise Father who wants to protect your heart.

Identity and Orientation

I want to offer a brief word about gender identity and sexual orientation. Many others have devoted themselves to understanding and mediating the complex issues of sexuality. I do not claim any expertise in this area, but I would like to share a few personal insights.

I have a great deal of compassion for those who are struggling with gender identity issues. I count among personal friends and acquaintances dozens who have assumed alternate identities and lifestyles. I struggled with gender issues in my teen years for a couple reasons.

First, as I have mentioned before, I grew up hungry for physical affection, and those longings were focused mostly toward my mom. I wanted hugs from a woman! If I had been exposed to lesbian activity as a young teenager, I may well have chosen that path. I had some leanings in that direction, and I would have been a target (and perhaps a victim) of today's agendas. The permissions and pressures of a society powerfully influence its young people. The sexual revolution has opened doors, created desires, and pressured today's teens in ways destructive to their hearts. The pressure is even trickling down to our preteens and young children who should not even have sex on their radar.

Second, I was such a tomboy! I wanted to play boys' sports (tackle football, please). I could throw a ball farther than many of the boys in my class. I wanted to take shop instead of sewing in school, but shop was offered only for boys. I spent my babysitting money on a .30-30 rifle. I loved to go camping, hiking, and hunting. I spent plenty of time seriously wishing I were a boy.

Assumptions regarding gender roles have changed drastically since I was in school, and much of it is for the better. Rigid stereotypes like those I grew up with can play a role in gender confusion. The fact that a girl wants to go hunting or a boy would rather play the flute than football has nothing to do with sexuality. A man can be sensitive and a woman can be athletic without challenging their God-given gender.

However, if I had been bombarded with the message that God might have made a mistake and it would be fine for me to decide to be a boy, there was a season in my life where I may have chosen that. There was no way I as a teenager could have understood the deep ramifications of such a choice. I am so thankful I didn't have enough information or opportunity to pursue that desire!

There are many challenges to embracing and celebrating womanhood. The issues and circumstances that lead a woman to alternative sexual lifestyles and identities are varied. What we have observed, how we have been treated, what others have said, and cultural pressures can all influence our thoughts and feelings. I realize my own experiences are rather shallow compared to the gender dysphoria others have experienced. For them, the perceived incongruity between their physical bodies and their feelings leads them to believe there has been a mistake. Their hearts feel like aliens in their own bodies.

Whatever the source or expression, such identity issues are heartbreaking! Our hearts feel some things so deeply, we are convinced they are true. In desperate attempts, we work at aligning our world with our feelings. But as vital as the heart is, we must come to terms with the fact that our hearts can be deceived. God knows our feelings, and He cares about our pain and confusion. This is the reason He has given us His Word and His Spirit. It's the reason He calls us to love each other and walk with each other through our heart issues.

One isolated heart is easily deceived. One isolated heart easily becomes hopeless. If you are walking through sexual issues of any kind, please don't do it alone! God has equipped individuals and groups to minister freedom and wholeness to your heart. It's crucial to seek the truth together and ask the Lord to bring healing and revelation.

The Church must open its arms to those who are struggling. We must learn what it looks like to speak the truth in love. We must not condone forbidden behavior, but it is not our job to condemn. A person who struggles with sexual issues is no more a sinner than the rest of us with our various struggles. Let's take each other's hands and trust Jesus for the whole hearts we so desperately desire.

My reading of the Bible paints a clear picture of God's wisdom and intentionality in creating male and female. Attempting to blur the lines and downplay the differences goes against all our Creator has revealed about Himself and us. And it lies to us about our identity, our value, and the goodness of God.

Jesus's Healing Extends to Our Sexuality

If all our secrets were laid bare, none of us could claim sexual purity. Most of us have experienced some sort of sexual activity that has injured our hearts. A naïve engagement with pornography, various kinds of experimentation, a "casual" romp, an emotional relationship that has gone too far, the giving of ourselves to buy a favor, or even committing outright rape and abuse. . . the list goes on and on.

But there is hope and healing for sexual brokenness! The Enemy lies to us about sexual activity, then condemns us when we follow his lead. Satan wants us to believe we're too broken and it's too late. But "we're too broken and it's too late" is *never* true—in sexual matters or any other.

In Chapter 6, I offered an expanded phrasing of Luke 19:10: "The Son of Man came to seek, find, save, heal, and restore that which was lost, destroyed, marred or dead." That is good news for our sexuality. The saving grace of Jesus brings us forgiveness, healing, and restoration. I would like to add another promise at this point: "Therefore, if anyone is in Christ, he is a new creation. The old has passed away; behold, the new has come" (2 Corinthians 5:17, ESV).

Please take time to let this sink in. When you accept Jesus's gift of grace, your past is forgiven. Your citizenship is transferred to a new kingdom, and the Holy Spirit takes up residence in you to bring power for healing and restoration. Add to all that this promise: you are a new creation. New! You do not get a new coat of paint to hide old stuff. You do not get new talking points about yourself. You *become* new: unused, unworn, unblemished.

You are no longer defined by your past. You are not defined by your desires. You are defined by God's new life in you. Hearts don't heal instantly; desires don't change instantly. You are not alone to figure this new person out. He who has saved you—and has set these sexual boundaries—will never leave you as you navigate these confusing, stormy waters. He is full of grace and healing and will lead you one step at a time. I pray He will give you grace to say no to every temptation. May He lead you to compassionate and gifted people to walk with you through those lonely places where you have been unable to find victory in your sexual journey.

In its proper context, sex is meant for our good, our pleasure, and our joy. The power and complexities of this force are unlike any other. May we all pursue and experience deep intimacy with Jesus as we press into Him for the ability to pursue whole hearts in the context of these realities.

Chapter 15 Reflection

1. Take some time to talk to the Lord about what you have read in this chapter.

   How is your heart responding?

   _____

   _____

   _____

   What questions do you have?

   _____

   _____

   _____

   Where do you feel helpless, or hopeless, or condemned?

   _____

   _____

   _____

2. Invite Jesus's love, comfort, and counsel into your sexual identity and activity, and ask Him to lead you. The Enemy may try to heap shame on you, but the Lord does not condemn; He helps those who ask.

   _____

   _____

   _____

   _____

Chapter 16

Marriage

To marry or not to marry? This is a huge question for women today. In cultures where women have few rights, marriage is a given and a necessity. But we in the West live in a time and place where most women can lead independent lives. We can get an education. We can work and have our own bank accounts. We can buy and sell homes. We can sign our own legal documents. We have freedom and autonomy that women in other times and cultures couldn't imagine.

This current reality may give one pause in considering marriage. *Why should I give up my freedom to commit myself to a man I don't need?* you may wonder. In today's culture, it is perfectly acceptable to live with a romantic partner without making a commitment. We can share resources, responsibilities, and good times until it gets too difficult, then leave and care for ourselves again. If we get married, it makes the process of separation too troublesome. So, why bother?

Those who follow Jesus and do not give themselves the option of trying things out for a while have other fears to weigh: *How can I be sure this is the right man? What if I commit myself, and we end up miserable? I'll be stuck for life in a situation in which I will never be happy. I can be friends with guys, but I'd rather remain celibate and independent. Marriage is not worth the risk.*

The concept of marriage has become divisive and controversial. But if we are women committed to truth, then we must shun all the wisdom of the world and look to our Father to define marriage for us.

God's Plan for Marriage

God spoke about marriage from the beginning: "Therefore a man shall leave his father and his mother and hold fast to his wife, and they shall become one flesh" (Genesis 2:24, ESV).

This verse begins with the word "therefore." In other words, this isn't a statement without context; it refers to *why* God ordained marriage in the first place. And the reason goes back a few verses. Earlier in this chapter, we learned that God began by creating a single human, Adam, and by declaring it was "not good" for this one person to be alone (see Genesis 2:18). God removed part of Adam and formed it into a woman. Adam recognized what had happened and declared, "This is bone of my bones and flesh of my flesh" (Genesis 2:23).

"Flesh of my flesh" means just that: body of my body, skin of my skin. But the Hebrew for "bone of my bones" has a broader meaning: essence of my essence, life of my life, strength of my strength. And what was the essence of Adam, the core of his identity? The image of God! This very life and essence of mankind now appeared in two forms. Adam was now face-to-face with a complementary, interdependent "other." And *therefore*, the two—the man and the woman—will become one. The image of God is reflected in this unity.

The Apostle Paul goes one step further, defining marriage as a reflection of the union between the church—the bride of Christ—and Jesus: "'Therefore a man shall leave his father and mother and hold fast to his wife, and the two shall become one flesh.' This mystery is profound, and I am saying that it refers to Christ and the church" (Ephesians 5:31-32, ESV).

Paul calls this a profound mystery, and my purpose is not to try to understand it all. But we dare not ignore the things that *are* clear: marriage is designed to be between a man and a woman, and God Himself makes them one. Our inner fountains of *thought* and *purpose* can grasp these things. But what about those *passions*?

In matters of romantic love, our hearts are vulnerable and easily deceived. We need to take a serious look at the concept of romance—that sense of mystery and excitement in the attraction between a man and a woman. Romance is a big deal for most women, and it is awakened and informed from an early age by fairy tales and Hollywood. Who among us has not at some time wished to be a beautiful princess rescued and adored by a handsome hero? Who has not dreamed of happily ever after?

Romance is at the heart of the universe. The story of creation, from beginning to end, is the story of a Father preparing a bride for His Son. Our hearts were created for this romance, and marriage is intended to illustrate it. We'll talk more about that in a later chapter. But for now, we must realize this romance is a far cry from the concoctions of authors and filmmakers.

The Rightful Role of Romance

Our culture has reduced "romance" to unthinking, uninformed feelings that awaken our passion without engaging our thought or purpose.

For too many women, romantic feelings are primary motivators, and emotions become the center of the decision-making process. Some confidently commit to their fairy-tale world, trusting themselves and their beloved to keep the romantic fires burning forever. Others fear the end of the dream so much, they don't dare engage in it. Many choose the middle ground, hoping the dream will last but remaining strapped to the ejection seat in case it doesn't work out.

In our relationships with men, we must put "romance" in its proper place in our hearts. A key problem is that romance is easily confused with genuine love. It is important for us to distinguish between the two. Romance is a feeling fed by treasured times together, shared interests, physical chemistry, the joy of being desired and treated well, and emotional intimacy. But no matter how hard you try, those glorious feelings will not last forever. If a man and a woman are not committed to staying together for better or for worse, the relationship will end when those feelings cannot be sustained. Romance is by no means a bad thing, but it is a distant second to the kind of sacrificial love and commitment that will sustain a marriage for the long haul.

It's important to engage the *whole* heart in these matters. We have defined the heart as *the inner fountain of passion, thought, and purpose.* If you understand your heart only as the center of feelings, and you define love as only a feeling, then you set yourself up for painful disappointment. Romance is certainly a subset of *passion*, but we must also engage *thought* and *purpose* in our romantic relationships.

Feelings are not bad things. God feels things, and we have been given the privilege of enjoying this aspect of His character. Our relationships with God certainly will include times of glorious intimacy and emotion. But here's the problem: feelings alone cannot be trusted because they are hopelessly fickle. Even a relationship with God that is based solely on feelings can be shaken and undermined. Any permanent relationship is a matter of choice and commitment.

What endears someone to you today may be the very thing that irritates you tomorrow. That warm, satisfied feeling you have now may vanish in an hour. Feelings can be influenced by circumstances, hormones, health, the weather, or what you had for breakfast! Feelings are hopelessly undependable. If you are relying solely on feelings, then what will you do when those warm fuzzies are gone? What if they are replaced by feelings of bitterness, or hopelessness, or weariness, or boredom?

It is not my intent to scare you away from marriage. Quite the opposite! My desire is to give you a sober and holy view of marriage. Marriage is intended to be an incredible blessing to both husband and wife. Consider two people who will give themselves sacrificially to promote each other. Two people who are committed to the restoration of each other's hearts. Two people who stand unified against the Enemy's attempts at destroying either of them. Two people, hand in hand, trusting God together.

Marriage is the only context God has planned for multiplying and filling the earth. The sex drive is intended to motivate us toward marriage. The desire to bear and nurture children is a God-given incentive toward marriage. God's plans for most of us will include marriage.

My husband and I have been married for over forty years, and it is not our feelings that have sustained us. We are still together because we gave ourselves no other option. Romance comes and goes, and there are times when all we can do is grit our teeth and ask the Lord for the grace to go on. And He is always faithful! The comfort, peace, and satisfaction we now share came at a high cost to our egos and our entitlements. Neither of us could have imagined what we were in for at the beginning. But our present good times are so much better than we could have imagined during our romantic beginnings! As we let ourselves be transformed by the difficult choices, and as we watch God faithfully give us the grace and power to continue, our hearts are enlarged and at rest.

Marriage is a good, good thing. But it is crucial for women to take a serious look at it, away from the fairy-tale visions. If you are feeling swept off your feet, consider where your feet are. They are not on solid ground! Give yourself time to hear from God, and from the people He has positioned to speak into your life.

And please, *please* hear the wisdom of God: "Do not be yoked together with unbelievers. For what do righteousness and wickedness have in common? Or what fellowship can light have with darkness?" (2 Corinthians 6:14). This command of God (like all the others) is grounded in His loving care for your heart. If you become one with someone who has not been restored to fellowship with God, then you will have two entirely different responses to hard times. Your decisions will be informed by different sets of values. Your resources actually come from different kingdoms. The ability to join hands and seek God *together* is indispensable. A man who does not seek first the kingdom of God will not have access to the wisdom or strength to move forward victoriously. You will have joined yourself to a deceived man.

Yes, marriage is at times difficult, but it is glorious. It may well be the greatest challenge *and* the greatest joy of your life. You will be called on to love unconditionally, give generously, serve selflessly, and forgive lavishly. In short, the Potter will throw you on His wheel and shape you into the image of Christ. You can trust Him to use marriage for your good and His glory!

Marrying and Not Marrying Are Both Walks of Faith

Marriage is, among other things, a great act of faith. But be careful where you place your faith! Do not expect marriage to be the solution to the needs of your heart. Do not place your hopes for wholeness in your husband. Men and women who come into marriage trusting a spouse to meet their deepest needs are sure to be disappointed. Marriage was never intended to take the place of dependence on God. But a man and a woman who bring their wounded and needy hearts to Jesus together will find healing and blessing.

A husband and wife are in a unique position to pray for and fight for each other's wholeness. The process is not easy. You may suffer because of your husband's brokenness and immaturity (and he will surely suffer because of yours). But, as you trust your heart to the master Potter, these difficulties will sanctify your own heart rather than injure it. A man and a woman committed to the healing of each other's hearts will find healing for their own as well. The complementary union of your hearts and lives will enable you as a couple to bear fruit neither of you could produce on your own. Marriage is intended to advance the Kingdom in your community and in the world.

However, there *will be* those of you who, for one reason or another, will not get married. Scripture clearly promotes singleness as well. Paul makes a strong case for staying single to serve God without distraction:

> *I would like you to be free from concern. An unmarried man is concerned about the Lord's affairs—how he can please the Lord. But a married man is concerned about the affairs of this world—how he can please his wife—and his interests are divided. An unmarried woman or virgin is concerned about the Lord's affairs: Her aim is to be devoted to the Lord in both body and spirit. But a married woman is concerned about the affairs of this world—how she can please her husband. I am saying this for your own good, not to restrict you, but that you may live in a right way in undivided devotion to the Lord.*
>
> *(1 Corinthians 7:32-35)*

If you choose singleness, or if singleness appears to be God's plan for you, Jesus promises blessing in that as well! Do not feel condemned or let yourself be pressured by those who claim to know the will of God for you. But neither disdain marriage. Let's not take Paul's admonition as a reason to disregard the rest of Scripture. Scripture must be embraced in its entirety, and it is never safe to cling to one passage without weighing it in light of the whole context. It is still not good for a man to be alone. Scripture promotes, blesses, and proclaims marriage as a foundational piece of life on the earth, but it *also* promotes and blesses singleness.

I have a special place in my heart for those who are single and don't want to be. If you are one of those women, I encourage you to take your heart to Jesus and let Him be Lord of your situation. Your heart will require comfort and wisdom, and He promises both. Your heart will require supernatural provision, whether it is the providing of a husband or the providing of the grace to remain contentedly single. It is vitally important to guard your heart during this time. Do not let the Enemy bring fear, rejection, or shame! Those things can easily motivate you toward a hurried and unwise decision. Stay close to Jesus and let His peace rule in your heart.

The biblical promises addressed to widows apply to all single women. Here are a couple for you to claim as your own:

> *A father to the fatherless, a defender of widows, is God in his holy dwelling.*
>
> (Psalm 68:5)

> *Blessed are those whose help is the God of Jacob, whose hope is in the LORD their God. . . The LORD watches over the foreigner and sustains the fatherless and the widow.*
>
> (Psalm 146:5,9)

Do not be afraid to ask boldly for a husband! Then allow God to enable you to remain thankful in your current circumstances. Trust Him for clarity and provision as you move forward. But remember that God's provision will never include something that contradicts His desire for you to remain pure and devoted to Him.

Marriage and singleness each have blessings for your heart. Each will challenge your heart. Whatever your current situation, commit your *inner fountain of passion, thought, and purpose* to the One who created you and loves you. He will use both the blessings and the challenges to heal and enlarge your heart.

Chapter 16 Reflection

Take time to share your heart with the Lord. Whether you are in a disappointing or difficult marriage, or have a history of marriage failure, or are still waiting for a husband, God has wisdom and comfort for you. And, if you are in a great marriage, ask Him to show you how to be a part of making it even better.

_____

_____

_____

_____

_____

_____

_____

_____

_____

_____

_____

_____

_____

_____

Motherhood

More and more women have been choosing to have fewer and fewer babies. Reasons may vary from woman to woman, but underlying it all is the strategic ploy of the Enemy to devalue both motherhood and children. Ultimately, it is an attack on the value of life itself. Reproduction and motherhood are at the core of God's command to be fruitful, multiply, and fill the earth.

An honest look at the female body makes my point. This body was designed to carry and feed a baby! A woman is vastly more than just a physical body, and motherhood is not all we were designed for. But let's not fail to honor the anatomy or the purpose for which it was designed!

The devaluing of motherhood is a direct attack on women's hearts. The yearning for motherhood is woven into the fabric of a woman's heart. This desire to bear children, as with all the other unique qualities God gives a woman, will not be equally dominant in everyone. But it is part of the heart of a woman, and the Enemy's unmistakable strategy is to manipulate a woman's *inner fountain of passion, thought, and purpose* away from motherhood. This strategy must be exposed and opposed!

God has not given us all the same level of desire for motherhood, and He never places our individual value on our bearing of children. But His treasuring of motherhood and babies must never take second place in the discussion.

The world would have us see our value in terms of our ability to contribute financially, intellectually, socially, and politically. We are easily drawn into this temptation to judge ourselves based on the worldly increase we bring! Getting an education, starting a career, and moving up the ladder are often promoted above motherhood as goals for successful women, and a baby is seen as a hindrance to these goals. This value system encourages us to delay marriage, delay having a baby, and— in its most horrific conclusion—abort a baby if it shows up unbidden. Lord Jesus, forgive us!

Preserving the Value of Motherhood

And after the baby arrives, then what? The legitimate option to give up a career and devote oneself to raising children has been disgracefully described as being "*just* a mom." We might as well make ridiculous statements like, "Jeff Bezos is *just* the founder of Amazon," or, "Francis is *just* the Pope." And if you think I am exaggerating for the sake of effect, I am not! There is not one mother (or one baby) less significant than either Jeff Bezos or Pope Francis. Again, our value does not come from worldly position or gain: every life has immeasurable intrinsic value which comes from God alone. And the woman who nurtures a life is as significant as that life itself. You may be the mother of the next pope or the next billionaire entrepreneur, or you may be the mother of a mother. All hold equal value and significance in the eyes of God and in His plans.

The increasing availability of contraceptive options in the last several decades has changed the landscape for married couples. I am not making a case against contraception, but I'd like to change the tone of the conversation. It is now a given that we can get married and never worry about having babies. But babies are a natural outcome of marriage—by design! God *loves* children, and He has ordered the world so we must work hard *not* to have them. Please let your hearts be informed by God in discussions and decisions about contraception. He has wisdom for you personally (although never contrary to Scripture), and hearts willing to listen are postured to hear from Him.

Children and careers are not necessarily mutually exclusive. But the reality is that either one of them will take strength and time from the other. As you consider options regarding the timing of schooling, having babies, training, and professional advancement, please guard your heart from lies about your identity and value!

Financial needs are also a concern in this decision-making process. Again, we must fight the input and judgments of the world. Budget-writing and financial goals have a place, but they must always consider the intrinsic *value* of children as well. The world thinks we need a lot more money and financial security than people of faith should worry about! Again, please let your heart listen to God about motherhood in these discussions and decisions.

The Enemy does have some convincing arguments against childbearing. Motherhood is disruptive, inconvenient, and pull-your-hair-out frustrating. And it is very, very costly: it creates tension in marriages, challenges sleep patterns, strains budgets, and makes a mockery of our attempts at peace and order. There is something in us that desires ease and prosperity, but neither of those will satisfy our hearts. We must never lose sight of how much God treasures children, and how He has woven motherhood into our hearts. The difficulties are the very things that drive our desperate hearts into the presence of God and deepen our intimacy with Him.

Motherhood catapults us into situations which will bring out all our weaknesses, temptations, and self-centered desires. It challenges our ability to love, exposes our lack of wisdom, and stretches our hearts seemingly beyond their ability to understand or endure. In short, healthy motherhood requires us to become disciples of Jesus. It requires us to learn His ways, to walk in the love He has for us *and* our children, and to give and receive forgiveness over and over. It requires us to surrender our hearts and our children's hearts to Him, allowing Him to strengthen and enlarge them as we trust Him.

God Will Provide

Mothers must sit at Jesus's feet as His disciples did. A disciple turns to God, listens to His counsel, treasures His presence and comfort, seeks His wisdom, relies on His strength, and asks Him for miracles. Wait—did I say miracles? Yes! Never underestimate His desire to intervene miraculously for you and your child. Whether it's the need for your newborn to please sleep for two hours in a row, the desire for a prodigal to come home, or any of the heart-wrenching needs a mother will experience for the entire life of her child, turn to God first. Prayer is our first line of defense and the greatest power for change. God loves your child even more than you do. Keep asking, keep seeking, and keep knocking!

You and your child have the same Father on duty. God may not grant us the quick fix we desire, but He is listening and answering us as we turn to him in our struggles with motherhood. He may part the waters, or He may simply walk through those rough waters with us and our children. In either case, fear should not be granted any place in our hearts. God is faithful, and He promises to use our difficulties for our good and His glory.

If we try to navigate those rushing waters by leaping across rocks where He has not led us, we will find those rocks slippery and our footing treacherous. We cannot control everything. God does not promise an easy path; He promises to be with us. Our hearts and our children's hearts are safe when we allow Him to lead:

When you pass through the waters, I will be with you; and when you pass through the rivers, they will not sweep over you. When you walk through the fire, you will not be burned; the flames will not set you ablaze.

(Isaiah 43:2)

And we know that in all things God works for the good of those who love him, who have been called according to his purpose.

(Romans 8:28)

As mothers, our biggest need will be faith! Childhood is full of complexities, dilemmas, needs, and dangers which cannot be anticipated or avoided. One of the biggest dangers to a mother's heart will be fear, along with its accompanying desire to control. Oh, dear sister, learn to recognize these attacks on your heart! A mother's love wants to shield her child's heart, mind, and body. But this is mission impossible. Our children *will* experience heart-wrenching difficulties, and we must not model fear for them. We will avoid many pitfalls by following God's wisdom in life's circumstances, but He never promises us or our children an easy life. Our children must learn, as must we, that problems are opportunities to grow and trust God. Control belongs to God, and fear is the realm of the Enemy. Neither fear nor control has a valid place in a mother's heart.

Motherhood not only presses us into discipleship, but also anoints us as disciple-makers. If you are a mom, your most important service to the Kingdom of God is training your children to know God, learn His Word, hear His voice, and trust Him in all circumstances. I can think of no visible position—in the Church or in the world—with the power to affect a life as much as the unsung mother in the obscurity of her home. No Hollywood hero can influence the world as much as a godly mom.

There will be times (lots of them!) of incredible self-sacrifice, from the moment we take that cute little baby home until the moment Jesus takes us home. But self-sacrifice is not destructive to our hearts. In fact, we are called to self-sacrifice, and Jesus is our example: "Then Jesus told his disciples, 'If anyone would come after me, let him deny himself and take up his cross and follow me'." (Matthew 16:24, ESV)

As mothers, we encounter many situations where we must choose to deny ourselves. And as we surrender our own comfort and desires, allowing Him to speak, provide, and enable, our hearts come under His healing, transforming influence.

Motherhood also fills our lives with immeasurable physical, emotional, and spiritual blessings. Nothing compares to the wonder of feeling a new life growing in a tummy, welcoming that new life into the world, and holding that dependent little stranger for the first time. The privilege of partnering with God in molding a young life and the adventure of watching that life unfold are unimaginably fulfilling. Spontaneous hugs, silly questions, toothless smiles, and the tender love that surprises you even on your worst day—there are priceless rewards awaiting a mom. And let's not overlook God's plan for our older years, when children and grandchildren become an incredible source of joy and provision.

The Pain of Infertility

There is another side to this matter: the heartbreaking experience of women who want to become moms and have physically not been able to. If you are among them, please do not let the Enemy bring devastation to your heart. Take your mourning and disappointment to God and let Him comfort you. He knows your pain and does not condemn you for it! In a perfect world, the tragedy of a barren womb would not exist. But as we've discussed before, we live in a fallen world and heartache awaits us all in one circumstance or another. Don't let the Enemy heap shame on you, and don't let your heart believe you are purposeless.

In some cultures, a woman's value actually *is* based on her bearing of children. Children in some cultures are considered assets, often because of the financial gain they represent, especially in agrarian societies. Having more children means having more *workers*! This, too, is a perversion, and it assaults the hearts of both mother and child. A woman's value is *not*, under any circumstances, based on how many children she has any more than a child's value is related to his or her ability to contribute to the family's resources. Both of these are lies of the Enemy!

Other women may suffer this same feeling when they look around them and see what seems like "everyone" having children and experiencing motherhood, when they are not. Regardless of the backstory, the temptation is to feel "less than," if we are childless or don't have as many children as we would like. This, too, is a lie of the Enemy.

Motherhood is not the only opportunity for a woman to give of herself and find purpose and meaning. If that door is not opening for you, trust the Lord to care for your heart and show you the next step. He has plans we have not even begun to imagine! As Jeremiah 29:11 reminds us, "'For I know the plans I have for you,' declares the LORD, 'plans to prosper you and not to harm you, plans to give you hope and a future.'"

Again, don't be afraid to ask for a miracle! We shy away from asking for miracles, because we are afraid of the disappointment that may come if they don't happen. I encourage you, dear sister, to entrust your heart to Jesus and ask boldly! We will never see miracles if we don't ask our Father for them! Faith invites us to ask for miracles and to place our hearts in the Father's hands amid the mystery. He can do "immeasurably more than all we ask or imagine" (see Ephesians 3:20)!

A woman's quest for identity and fulfillment is fueled by the nature of her heart. And a woman's heart is, by design, a nurturing heart. The desire for motherhood flows from this nurturing heart. That's why I would like to conclude this chapter by honoring all the other ways a woman brings the love of God to her world by being a nurturer.

God is a nurturer. He initiates relationship. He moves into our pain. He carries our sorrows. He desires our peace and joy, and His heart is grieved as He walks with us through injustices and foolishness. He brings comfort, counsel and understanding. He brings *Himself.* He makes His heart vulnerable to ours. And there is a huge deposit of this attribute of God in the hearts of women. We are nurturers.

Being a nurturer is costly. It takes up time and resources, and it makes your heart vulnerable to another's pain. Yet it also brings great joy and satisfaction. As you step into nurturing roles, you are not guaranteed a happy outcome. You may never even know the outcome. But I encourage you to let the Lord use you as a nurturer. It requires strength and courage. You will have to lean on the Lord for wise boundaries. Nurturing may look like giving a hug and an encouraging word to a stranger whom you will never see again. It may look like opening your heart and home to the friends your kids hang out with. It may look like a long-term commitment to foster or adopt. It may look like taking younger women under your wing and encouraging their hearts. Or it may look like a complete role reversal as you care for an aging parent.

Let me say it again: Being a mother, along with its accompanying role of being a wife, is costly. Family is the primary crucible where the Kingdom of God is forged on the earth. Home is the first place where we begin to learn to deny ourselves. As mothers, we model it for our kids. First by example, and then with instruction, we show the next generation the grace and the joy of taking up our crosses daily.

A whole heart does not fear the cost to itself. As you ask God for the strength and wisdom to give yourself to those who need your presence and care, you open your heart to a supernatural touch from Him. Your fear of disappointment or rejection is transformed into wholehearted, selfless giving as you allow Him to love others through you. You become part of nurturing your own heart—and others' hearts—toward wholeness.

Chapter 17 Reflection

1. How has the world lied to you about the value of motherhood? Ask the Lord to speak significance into that role. And ask Him for wisdom in how to order *your* life around that reality. Do not try to order your choices by how someone else is doing it. If possible, take time to pray with your husband about these things.

_____

_____

_____

_____

2. Are you grieving barrenness, or the loss of a child? Allow yourself time to mourn and mend. Ask the God of all comfort into your pain.

_____

_____

_____

_____

3. Can you identify ways that the Lord has used you as a nurturer? Do you sense Him leading you to into a nurturing relationship?

_____

_____

_____

_____

Chapter 18

Authority and Submission

H ow did your heart respond when you saw the title of this chapter? Passions, thoughts, and purposes get highly energized when we start talking about the issues of authority and submission, whether in family, church, business, school, or government. Some hearts may hear domination and servitude. Others may hear power and weakness. Privilege and deprivation. Advantage and disadvantage. Freedom and bondage.

Most of our angst about this can be attributed to a wrong understanding and a misuse of authority, bringing fear and confusion. But we cannot have whole hearts without finding rest and peace in God's intentions for authority and submission. We must guard our hearts from judging God's ways by how they have been wrongly interpreted and exercised. Our hearts must grapple with this issue and come to a knowledge of the truth.

We must deal with authority and submission precisely because we are made in God's image. It is part of what it means to have an *inner fountain of passion, thought, and purpose.* No other living thing in creation *chooses* to submit or to lead. In other species, dominance depends on instinct, circumstance, or brute force. Humans are the only ones whose hearts must wrestle with this issue. Only humans can choose servant leadership. Only humans can submit as an ultimate act of their God-given authority to choose! As God's image bearers, we can *choose*, by His grace and for His glory, to lead or to follow according to His design.

The core issue here has been the same since Eden. Power. Control. Leadership. Adam and Eve chose to ignore the leadership of God. Satan tempted them to make their own decisions about good and bad, right and wrong. They saw the opportunity to be in control and they grabbed it. It is the same for all of us to one degree or another. We like to be in charge. We *love* to be in charge. Our hearts are motivated to watch out for themselves by ruling in their world.

But there is a serious problem with the fallen desire to rule: it is universally self-promoting. One person's desire to rule inevitably conflicts with another's. The desire for power starts wars, ruins marriages and families, divides churches, destroys businesses, and in general wreaks havoc on the earth. As women, we must be prepared to deal knowledgably and wisely with this dynamic.

Who's in Charge Here, Anyway?

God is not surprised by the destructive potential of power. He is, in fact, the source of all power, and He understands its dangers. Only in the Godhead is power exercised perfectly and peacefully. We find in Him our perfect model for authority and submission, and we find in His Word wisdom and clarity as our hearts grapple with the issues of leading and following.

The Father, the Son, and the Holy Spirit are all God. They all carry the same authority. They are all equal in essence and glory. Not one is more important or more worthy than the other two. *But*. . . they differ in roles and authority. We spoke in Chapter 5 about how the Creation was a united activity of the Godhead. They acted in unison. But despite their identity as one, submission exists in the Godhead.

Jesus submits to the Father. The Father *sent* Him into the world. Jesus never sends the Father anywhere. And when Jesus agonized in the Garden of Gethsemane, asking the Father if there were another way for His will to be accomplished, Jesus ended His request with total submission: "Father, if you are willing, take this cup from me; yet not my will, but yours be done"(Luke 22:42.)

The Holy Spirit is sent by Jesus. Jesus tells his disciples, "It is for your good that I am going away. Unless I go away, the Advocate will not come to you; but if I go, I will send him to you" (John 16:7).

This mutual submission does not diminish the glory of any member of the Godhead, nor does it elevate any One above the other. It provides the context for them to honor each other and act in unity.

The same is true for mankind. To begin to consider authority and submission in a healthy way, we must adjust our *passions, thoughts, and purposes* to align with truth. Neither authority nor submission has anything to do with our significance. The value of each of us is not contingent on our getting to be in charge. Leadership roles are just that—*roles*, not badges of importance. Subordinate and supportive roles are *roles*, not signs of inferiority.

Jesus addressed this issue emphatically with His disciples. He clearly challenged their hearts and minds to redefine power and significance. He told them, "You know that those who are regarded as rulers of the Gentiles lord it over them, and their high officials exercise authority over them. Not so with you. Instead, whoever wants to become great among you must be your servant, and whoever wants to be first must be slave of all." (Mark10:42-44)

The Bible gives another caution to those who have a desire to rule. The writer of Hebrews says that leaders "keep watch over you as those who must give an account" (Hebrews 13:17a). In other words, leaders are stewards who must answer to God about how they use their authority! These are sobering words. Those who find themselves in positions of authority are answerable to God for how well they *serve* those under them!

What about those of us who have someone in authority over them? Our submission is also connected to our relationship with the Lord: "Submit yourselves [to the authority of] every human institution *for the sake of the Lord [to honor His name]*" (1 Peter 2:13, AMP, emphasis mine). And, we are called on to care for our leaders, for their sake as well as for ours: "Obey them so that their work will be a joy, not a burden, for that would be of no advantage to you" (Hebrews 13:17b).

This biblical view of authority and submission challenges the natural inclinations of fallen humanity. Unredeemed hearts want their own way. This is universal in all relationships, but the subject has been particularly contentious concerning relationships between men and women. We as women must sift through the controversy and have clarity on God's design for men and women to be unified in their position as stewards and image bearers on the earth.

Where the Tension Began

It began with Adam and Eve. It was not a unified mankind that chose self-rule. Adam and Eve did not confer together on a plan. Eve made her own decision. Adam made his own decision. And then neither of them owned up to it! Adam blamed Eve, and Eve blamed the serpent. Two hearts, ripped from their fellowship with God by their own choices, neither able to acknowledge the truth.

Genesis 3 goes on to describe the severe consequences of this incident, known as the Fall, for the man, for the woman, and for the serpent. Let's focus on what the Lord said to Eve. Please take time with me to again take a detailed look at this passage and its context. There are core truths here we must understand and embrace:

> *To the woman he said, "I will make your pains in childbearing very severe; with painful labor you will give birth to children. Your desire will be for your husband, and he will rule over you."*
>
> *(Genesis 3:16)*

In this passage, there are two consequences spoken to the woman. The first has to do with the physical challenges of pregnancy and birth. Many of us have experienced that reality, and I will not expound on it. The second has to do with the relationship between man and woman, and we need to have a serious look at this.

"Your desire will be for your husband ["man" in Hebrew], and he will rule over you." Let's remember the context of this statement. This is not a command for us to follow or a description of how things ought to be. This is a picture of the dysfunction that is the result of Adam and Eve's sin in the garden. This is a curse.

To get a better sense of the tone of these words, I want to look at a verse in the next chapter, which uses the same two verbs—"desire" and "rule"—in a parallel context. This is the story of Cain, who was angry because the Lord did not look favorably on his offering. The Lord gave him a stern warning: "Sin is crouching at your door; it desires to have you, but you must rule over it." (Genesis 4:7)

Sin desires to *have* Cain. This is not the Hebrew word we would use if we wanted to "have" a vacation, or a friend. Here, the Hebrew "have" suggests vicious intent. This word can be described as the desire of a wild animal to devour its prey. Sin wants to control, dominate, and devour Cain.

When we plug this understanding into our verse about Eve, it totally changes the tone. This is not a picture of a wife with positive longings for her beloved husband. Rather, it suggests she will have the urge to control, manipulate, or destroy Adam: "Your desire will be for your husband."

When Eve gave in to Satan, there was birthed in her (and the women who would follow) a desire to control or "devour" man. And women since then have been born under this curse, which feeds our discontent with God's design for us.

This explains a lot of what we see in the world today. The curse elicits thoughts and behaviors that either subtly or overtly promote women as more capable, more necessary, and more powerful than men. It is easy to see these attitudes among women simply as an understandable reaction to their historical subjugation. But the root is deeper and goes all the way back to the Garden. We were born under a curse that drives our hearts toward desires to put down and dominate rather than to complement and cooperate. There is a propensity toward independence rather than interdependence. And all this brings conflict, confusion, and dysfunction to homes, businesses, churches, and societies.

Please don't take offense. I am not making personal accusations against you. I am not disparaging women in general. I am defining the battle that is before us. It will affect some women more than others, but our *inner fountains of passion, thought, and purpose* exist under the influence of this curse. We might not act on this desire to dominate men, but we must be aware of this tendency in and among us.

Influence over Control

The other part of the verse affects women globally and individually. "He will *rule over* you." Ruling, like desiring, can be either a legitimate position from God or a destructive distortion of God's intent. God made Joseph a ruler in Egypt, and it was a good thing! David ruled over Israel, and it was a blessing for him and for the nation. God rules over everything, and that is our confidence!

But ruling can take the form of subjugation, suppression, and repressive control. In our parallel verse, Genesis 4:7, this is exactly the kind of ruling God told Cain to exercise over sin! It is crucial that man give sin no influence in his life. He must never entertain it, or partner with it in any way. He must suppress and subdue the influence of sin in his life.

But this is not the right relationship between man and woman! Influencing and partnering with each other *should* characterize relationships between men and women. This curse of the Fall is the evil distortion of God's design for man and woman.

To summarize, I would like to restate our two verses.

- Regarding the *right* relationship between mankind and sin in Genesis 4:7: "Sin desires to destroy you by controlling and manipulating how you think and what you do. But you must exercise absolute control over it and give it no voice or influence in your life."
- Regarding the *cursed* relationship between man and woman in Genesis 3:16: "The desire of woman will be to step out of a complementary relationship, and to control and manipulate man. Man will want to exercise absolute control, disdaining and ignoring woman's essential complementary role."

Now I likely have everybody mad at me! Listen carefully, please. I am not making a statement about anyone's personal character. I am not lumping all men into one batch of power-hungry misogynists. I am not characterizing all women as manipulative and controlling. I am saying this curse is alive and well in today's fallen world, and we need to be aware of how it has influenced our views of authority and submission. We cannot discount the fact that this curse has affected all of us, both in how we have acted and how we have been treated.

Our hearts, those *inner fountains of passion, thought, and purpose,* must be rewired by God's design for healthy interdependent relationships. We must repent when we have been wrong and forgive when we have been wronged. Our hearts *can* come to a healthy understanding of authority and submission between men and women.

It's important to also look at another side of this breakdown in the understanding of man-woman relationships. There is an another lie the Enemy has snuck into the world. This is the lie that women should, in fact, be passive, quiet, and resigned. Women who believe this are afraid to be strong, gifted, or well educated.

This lie ignores the complementary man-woman relationship God ordained at the beginning. Adam did not need a little helper to take care of mundane stuff so he could take his rightful place as caretaker of the earth and image bearer of God. The call to be caretakers and image bearers is on *all* of mankind. Ladies, dare to be strong and gifted. Dare to believe those powerful dreams the Lord has given you. But please pursue those dreams in a way that honors God *and* honors men. Do not be a combatant in the gender wars. If your dreams include a desire to prove the superiority of women, or to put men down, then those dreams are not from God.

The Path of Honor

Marriage is an obvious place where the curse from Genesis 3:16 is likely to rear its ugly head. It is a place where the Enemy wants to bring confusion and frustration. Let's step back and see how roles of authority and submission within a marriage are practical ways the Lord has given us to move forward in peace and unity. God has given a clear picture of the working relationships in a family:

> *Wives, submit yourselves to your husbands, as is fitting in the Lord. Husbands, love your wives and do not be harsh with them. Children, obey your parents in everything, for this pleases the Lord.*
> *(Colossians 3:18-20)*

As ones who submit to God, it is fitting for us wives to honor Him by honoring our husbands' leadership roles. Husbands are to love their wives as Christ loved the church, and children are to obey their parents. None of this will play out in perfect little vignettes. The husbands, the wives, and the children will all encounter difficulties. But that does not alter God's design. A husband is called to sacrificially love even an ungrateful, nagging, contentious, deceitful wife. A wife is called to submit to a husband who may not love her well and may choose to dominate rather than lead. But despite the messiness of it all, God will bring blessing to families who trust Him and submit their hearts for His help, healing, and transformation.

My submission to my husband does not diminish me any more than Jesus's submission to the Father diminishes Him. The God-assigned roles of authority and submission within a marriage do not set aside the cooperative and complementary partnership between husbands and wives. It is not God's intention to establish a unilateral dominance that ignores or negates the equally important wisdom of a wife. It is God's intention for a wife's heart to be engaged in partnering with her husband to pursue, discern, and carry out His plans for their marriage and family. God is not telling us to shut up and follow blindly. He is not advocating passivity.

But there will be times when consensus cannot be reached, and a decision must be made. God has ordained that, at these times, it is up to the husband to lead. And the wife's role is to yield, even as she respectfully protests.

And an even bigger "but". . . some husbands may not welcome or receive our input. What then? We *will* find ourselves in positions where our husbands either will not listen or cannot see our perspectives. We may see danger signals they don't see, and we may follow our husband's leadership straight into some negative consequences. In a fallen world, this is inevitable. But when we are following God's leadership, we can trust Him with the things that make no sense to us. He promises to work *all* things—even our husbands' mistakes—together for good!

I know these are difficult words for women who have suffered under cruel authority! And I want to make a couple things clear before I move on. These two things are not within the scope of this book, and I will not be expounding on them. But they are extremely important.

First, I am *not* suggesting a woman remain in a situation where she is being abused. If you or your children are not safe because of a man ruling over your life, please stop reading, get help, and get out.

Second, I am *not* suggesting we should avoid being active in pursuing justice around the issues of women and men in society. Some will be called to that, and I pray that God will grant them wisdom and favor as He uses them in that arena. But both the goals and the means of achieving them must flow from confidence in who we are and what God desires. True wisdom will bring a vision that elevates and honors both men and women. We were designed as coheirs and coworkers. We were meant to complement rather than compete.

Historically and culturally, there have been attacks on the roles and identities of men and women as God's intentions have been warped and manipulated. But this is not the Lord's heart, and we should not throw out the design because it has been twisted. Let's look at some truths about authority and submission:

- Authority and submission have a proper, healthy place in relationships among mankind. They are *not* a result of the Fall but were operating in the eternal Godhead before man was created.
- While there is much to be learned from the curse spoken to Eve, authority and submission are *not* gender roles. Authority is not restricted to men, and submission is not restricted to women. Both women and men can be leaders and followers.
- All women are not subject to all men. The scriptures that specifically talk about a woman's submission are concerned with wives submitting to their own husbands.
- Authority was given to *all mankind* at Creation. Men and women carry the same image of God, and their authority is rooted in their relationship to their Creator. They were given dominion over creation, not over each other.
- Authority is not a mark of superiority, and submission is not a sign of inferiority. Authority and submission are active in the Trinity, and there is neither superiority nor inferiority in the Godhead.
- Authority and submission are common in all of aspects of life. Leaders are necessary in business, family, government, finance, sports, education and more. Most leaders have colleagues or

partners who carry out their wishes. A good decision-maker will heed the input of colleagues, but if there is no consensus, *someone* must make the decision. This task is the role of leadership.

- God puts a high value on unity. But unity does not require us all to want the same thing or see things the same way. In a marriage, unity requires us to submit to each other and stand behind final decisions, *whether we agree with our spouse or not.* This is authority and submission in action.
- Submission is not the same as passivity! It does not mean we should keep our mouths shut or follow blindly. We should respectfully share our concerns as they arise.
- There is no earthly authority whom we should follow into sin. Never put the will of a husband, a boss, or anyone else above the will of God.

Not one of us is queen of the world. We all operate under authority of some kind, and God calls us to submit to them: "Let everyone be subject to the governing authorities, for there is no authority except that which God has established. The authorities that exist have been established by God" (Romans 13:1).

Who are the authorities in your life? Parents, teachers, bosses, government officials, a husband, pastors? Each of these has the power to bless your plans, and they have the power to hinder. They can protect you from moving forward in a foolish plan you have concocted, and they can obstruct the dream God has put in your heart! Some in authority may give you lots of freedom and help you along the way. Some, in their weakness or brokenness, may put up frustrating roadblocks. Some may understand your dreams and advocate for them. Some may be wiser than you and their caution will benefit you.

And here's the rub . . . you will not always know which is which! You may be certain your way is best and an authority figure is opposing you for their own selfish or foolish reasons. But you could be the one who is ill-informed, misguided, or motivated by selfishness. Our own hearts are so easily deceived!

King David provides a profound and challenging example of honoring authority. As a youth, he was anointed king by God's prophet Samuel. Even though he knew he had God's anointing on him, he continued to subject himself to his parents and then to Israel's unjust King Saul before the Lord made the way for him to assume the throne. He served his parents by watching over their sheep. Then he took a servant's role in the household of King Saul. *Then* he became a fugitive, pursued by the jealous Saul who wanted to kill him! Even when he had the opportunity to protect and promote himself by killing Saul, he did not take matters into his own hands. Instead, he chose to trust the Lord's timing for the promises that had been spoken over him. David's men encouraged him to kill Saul and take his rightful place as king, but he refused:

> He said to his men, "The LORD forbid that I should do such a thing to my master, the LORD's anointed, or lay my hand on him; for he is the anointed of the LORD."
>
> *(1 Samuel 24:6)*

David's submission freed him from trying to force God's plans to happen. He allowed the Lord to work out His plan in His time. And David guarded his heart during this season by choosing an attitude of faith towards God, and respect towards the person in authority. These are choices we can make despite our feelings or fears.

Leadership

Women are also called upon to take positions of leadership. Leadership is just as problematic as submission! It comes with just as many challenges to our hearts. A leader will be criticized, ignored, misunderstood, demeaned, lied about, opposed, resented, and vilified. Opposition can be hostile, and a leader may find herself in a very lonely position.

Our hearts will encounter temptations in leadership as well. An imperfect heart is prone to arrogance and self-preservation, and it is easy to go in a direction that injures oneself and others. We must not be quick to desire power!

What does wholehearted authority look like for those of you in leadership? It looks like *servanthood.* The purpose of authority is to use all your resources to serve others rather than to promote yourself:

> *Jesus called them and said, "You know that the rulers of the Gentiles lord it over them, and those in high positions use their authority over them. It must not be this way among you! Instead whoever wants to be great among you must be your servant, and whoever wants to be first among you must be your slave—just as the Son of Man did not come to be served but to serve, and to give his life as a ransom for many."*
>
> *(Matthew 20:25–28, NET)*

As one in authority, you are called to represent the authority (and therefore the character) of God in the situation you are in. God's authority is never separate from His character. It is never separate from His care for you and those under your leadership. It never cares for a task more than it cares for the hearts that are impacted.

And what does wholehearted submission look like? Again, it looks like servanthood. It's not just doing enough to keep the peace or to keep a job. Wholehearted submission means serving your leader by honoring their decisions and doing all you can to make them successful, whether you agree with them or not. Ultimately, your submission is an act of submission to God. You are honoring Him by cooperating with His design for earthly leadership. Submitting to someone in the position to direct your life in one way or another does not require all your confidence to be in that person. You can submit as an act of reverence toward God because you trust *Him* with the outcome.

God is more interested in the condition of our hearts than He is in how smoothly everything runs. Both leading and submitting will reveal places in our hearts where there is bitterness, self-centeredness, fear, or pride. Submission in particular can *feel* like it constricts and diminishes our hearts. But living under authority actually gives us the opportunity to let our hearts be enlarged and strengthened. Submission places our hearts in the hands of our God. He is the Potter who will use the challenges of submission to knead, soften, and mold us. Submission will require us to grow in humility and faith. As we wrestle with the wisdom of choices that make us unhappy or uncomfortable, we can quiet our hearts with this truth:

> *We are convinced that every detail of our lives is continually woven together to fit into God's perfect plan of bringing good into our lives, for we are his lovers who have been called to fulfill his designed purpose.*
>
> *(Romans 8:28, TPT)*

The Father, Son, and Holy Spirit serve each other—and us—by exercising their roles for the good of all. Whether we have a position of authority or of submission, we are to follow the Godhead's example in serving one another. Wholeheartedness in matters of authority will require us to engage our *inner fountains of passion, thought, and purpose* in trusting God more than we trust ourselves. Let's allow our hearts to lean into Him for the grace and wisdom to maintain actions and attitudes that are like His, whether we are leading or following.

Chapter 18 Reflection

1. How have your experiences with the authorities in your life spoken to you about your value—either positively or negatively?

_____

_____

_____

_____

2. In what specific ways do you see the need for you to trust God in a situation where you and a specific authority do not agree? Ask Him for wisdom and faith!

_____

_____

_____

_____

3. Do you sense the Lord inviting you to engage in the process of making an unhealthy environment more healthy for everyone involved? Spend time praying and listening about the situation. How can you begin to move forward in love and humility?

_____

_____

_____

_____

Part Six:
The Whole Picture

Chapter 19

Hearts Built Together

We have talked so far about our individual hearts. Your heart and my heart. But the picture is not complete until we remove the zoom lens and study the panoramic view. While the Lord's one-on-one ministry to our hearts is fundamental for each of us, we must not stop there. An isolated heart is not whole. God's final plan is not about a bunch of individuals. We can each receive comfort, healing, salvation, and restoration as individuals, but the work is completed only as our individual hearts connect to other hearts in God's eternal plan.

We have talked about your identity, but you as an individual are not meant to stand alone. You are part of something bigger than yourself. Bigger than your world. Bigger, even, than your lifetime. This is a profound and essential reality for your *inner fountain of passion, thought, and purpose* to take hold of in its journey to wholeness.

Your heart is unique. Others may appear to have similar passions, thoughts, or purposes, but only in you are they fashioned together in the specific ways that make you who you are. And that makes you the only person who fits into your spot in the bigger picture.

Jesus is not raising up a mass of independent wholehearted people. In fact, "independent" and "whole" are mutually exclusive when it comes to our hearts. Jesus is building a community of believers the Bible refers to as "the Church."

We Are His Church and His Body

The Bible has much to say about the Church, but I'll tell you one thing it does *not* say: it never refers to the Church as a physical meeting place. It is not a beautiful medieval cathedral or a repurposed theater like the building where I meet with other believers. The Church is not a *place*.

So what is it? Scripture uses three different pictures to describe the corporate identity of the Church: a dwelling, a body, and a bride. Let's look at these three identities.

God calls the Church His temple. Historically, the temple in Jerusalem was called the dwelling place of God. But God made it clear from the beginning that His dwelling would not be limited to a building. Stephen, a leader in the early Church, said:

> It was Solomon who built a house for him. However, the Most High does not live in houses made by human hands. As the prophet says: "Heaven is my throne, and the earth is my footstool. What kind of house will you build for me? says the Lord. Or where will my resting place be?"
>
> *(Acts 7:47-49)*

Where will His resting place be? In *us*! In His Church, the community of all believers. He has come to our individual hearts, but His desire is for our hearts to be built *together* into one glorious dwelling place for Him.

Do you not know that you [plural] are God's temple [singular] and that God's Spirit dwells in you [plural]?

(1 Corinthians 3:15, ESV)

In him the whole building is joined together and rises to become a holy temple in the Lord. And in him you [plural] too are being built together to become a dwelling in which God lives by his Spirit.

(Ephesians 2:21–22)

God's temple is holy, and you [plural] are that temple.

(1 Corinthians 3:17, ESV)

The second aspect of our identity is that of the body of Christ. We are not just the place where God rests; we are the place where God works. Believers are referred to corporately as His body—the vessel through which He continues to minister on the earth. One body, in all our different parts, working together to bring Jesus to our world:

For as in one body we have many members, and the members do not all have the same function, so we, though many, are one body in Christ, and individually members one of another.

(Romans 12:4–5, ESV)

One body made of members who belong to each other. This concept of a unified identity is foreign to today's popular values of individualism and self-sufficiency. This requires our hearts to embrace humility and vulnerability at a level most of us haven't begun to comprehend. We are God's one dwelling place, one body, and each of us is one piece of the whole.

In the above passage from Romans, Paul was speaking to believers—both Jews and Gentiles—who were living in Rome, a city he had not visited yet. So, when Paul says we are one body in Christ, he is not talking about a local church he is a part of. He is including himself and the Roman believers in a single universal entity. Paul expounds on this concept in his first letter to the believers in Corinth:

Just as a body, though one, has many parts, but all its many parts form one body, so it is with Christ. For we were all baptized by one Spirit so as to form one body—whether Jews or Gentiles, slave or free—and we were all given the one Spirit to drink. Even so the body is not made up of one part but of many.

Now if the foot should say, "Because I am not a hand, I do not belong to the body," it would not for that reason stop being part of the body. And if the ear should say, "Because I am not an eye, I do not belong to the body," it would not for that reason stop being part of the body. If the whole body were an eye, where would the sense of hearing be? If the whole body were an ear, where would the sense of smell be? But in fact God has placed the parts in the body, every one of them, just as he wanted them to be. If they were all one part, where would the body be? As it is, there are many parts, but one body.

The eye cannot say to the hand, "I don't need you!" And the head cannot say to the feet, "I don't need you!" On the contrary, those parts of the body that seem to be weaker are indispensable, and the parts that we think are less honorable we treat with special honor. And the parts that are unpresentable are treated with special modesty, while our presentable parts need no special treatment. But God has put the body together, giving greater honor to the parts that lacked it, so that there should be no division in the body, but that its parts should have equal concern for each other. If one part suffers, every part suffers with it; if one part is honored, every part rejoices with it.

Now you are the body of Christ, and each one of you is a part of it.

(1 Corinthians 12:12–27)

Consider the ramifications of these truths for your heart. You are not a stand-alone being. You have become part of a habitation God is building for Himself. You are one part of a whole body. You have a spot only you can fill. Your well-being and fruitfulness depend on other hearts and lives being pieced together.

This truth is crucial to our pursuit of whole hearts. Can you imagine a leg or a finger or an eye pursuing wholeness outside of the context of a functioning body? It is a silly concept. A leg was never made to function on its own. And the rest of the body needs that leg to be effective.

Someone missing a leg is handicapped. The Body of Christ without you is handicapped. You without the rest of the body are handicapped. Your heart alone is handicapped. We who are pursuing whole hearts must embrace this truth. It is much easier to concentrate solely on ourselves without considering the value of belonging and contributing, which require us to open our hearts and be vulnerable and interdependent.

Please let this truth speak to your heart about your value. There is a tendency in most of us to compare ourselves to others and conclude we are either inadequate and insignificant, or better qualified and more important. Inadequacy, insignificance, and pride are all mortal enemies of a whole heart. Comparison has no place among those who are equal contributors, in different capacities, to the whole.

Our hearts cannot stay in a safe cocoon alone with Jesus. They must embrace others and join themselves to broken brothers and sisters. A whole heart will cover the indignities and celebrate the successes of others. A whole heart will share the pain of another grieving heart. It will let itself be known, not hiding weaknesses or mistakes. No heart is meant to be isolated in its life experiences. A whole heart will embrace the ups and downs of the hearts around it.

This is a challenge for me. The ups and downs of my own heart are more than enough to walk through without having to take time for others' hearts. This "one body" stuff requires my passions, thoughts, and purposes to be enlarged and transformed. But that's what we're after, right? Those of us desiring whole hearts must walk in humility, compassion, generosity, forgiveness, and vulnerability on a whole new level.

We Are the Bride of Christ

Our unified, intertwined, interdependent hearts have a third corporate identity: The Bride. The Father is preparing a Bride for His Son. We are that Bride! In all the complexities of life, in all that has damaged our hearts and is healing our hearts, in all the Lord is doing to form and unite us as one, God is fashioning a Bride. From the Garden of Eden until now, and on until Jesus returns, this is the eternal plan. Jesus is coming back for His Bride. One Bride. I am not His Bride, and you are not His Bride. We, together with all His people before and after, are His Bride. A corporate identity, a unified heart.

This picture of Jesus and His Bride is meant to communicate the profound eternal nature of God's love and plan for our hearts. Our individual lives, our lives together, and the entire history of mankind are moving toward an eternity in which all hearts committed to Him will be united with His heart forever. Our passions, thoughts, and purposes will be one with His passions, thoughts, and purposes, and we will reign eternally with Him as His Bride: "Let us rejoice and be glad and give him glory! For the wedding of the Lamb has come, and his bride has made herself ready" (Revelation 19:7).

"The bride has made herself ready"? How do we get ready? By aligning our passions, thoughts, and purposes with His, by allowing Him to comfort, heal, and transform us individually, and then by pressing into Him as He unites us as one. It is in unity—with each other and with the Holy Spirit—that we cry out to Jesus for the fulfillment of all things: "The Spirit and the bride say, 'Come!'" (Revelation 22:17).

And Jesus answers us, "Yes, I am coming soon" (Revelation 22:20).

This unfathomable eternal plan was in place at Creation, but it has been a mystery even to God's servants, the angels. They watched in wonder as Adam and Eve gave their inheritance to Satan in the garden. They saw God choose Abraham to establish a new chosen nation. They watched as that fickle nation of Israel honored God, and then abandoned Him, repeating that cycle over and over throughout the centuries. They saw the Son of God descend to Earth as a man, and they watched in disbelief as He was killed on a cross!

And the angels watched as Jesus rose from the dead with a power that began to transform hearts. God is unveiling the mystery of this plan to His heavenly host as they watch the miraculous working of the Holy Spirit to make us one as His Church, His Body, and His Bride. Paul puts it this way in his letter to the Ephesians:

> *Although I am less than the least of all the Lord's people, this grace was given me: to preach to the Gentiles the boundless riches of Christ, and to make plain to everyone the administration of this mystery, which for ages past was kept hidden in God, who created all things. His intent was that now, **through the church,** the manifold wisdom of God should be made known to the rulers and authorities in the heavenly realms, according to his eternal purpose that he accomplished in Christ Jesus our Lord.*
>
> *(Ephesians 3:8–11, emphasis mine)*

The angels are watching us! They watch as our hearts are knit together. They watch as Jesus fashions and prepares each individual stone to be fit together with the others. They watch as the bride makes herself ready for her Lover. Paul goes on to pray for the church, asking that we, *together as one*, may be empowered to grasp the immensity of God's love:

> *For this reason I kneel before the Father, from whom every family in heaven and on earth derives its name. I pray that out of his glorious riches he may strengthen you with power through his Spirit in your inner being, so that Christ may dwell in your hearts through faith. And I pray that you, being rooted and established in love, may have power, together with all the Lord's holy people, to grasp how wide and long and high and deep is the love of Christ, and to know this love that surpasses knowledge— that you may be filled to the measure of all the fullness of God.*
> *(Ephesians 3:14–19)*

Rooting, grounding, and comprehending must happen in each of our hearts, but it is God's plan that the fullness of the knowledge of His love be revealed in our unity. He wants to fill us *as one* with all His fullness.

In the end, as he shares God's heart for us, Paul cannot help breaking into spontaneous worship. God, who came up with this unfathomable eternal plan and is making it happen, can certainly do far more than anything we can imagine. And the earth will be filled with His glory as the unified church rises to fulfill all His plans for her:

> *Now to him who is able to do far more abundantly than all that we ask or think, according to the power at work within us, to him be glory **in the church** and in Christ Jesus throughout all generations, forever and ever. Amen.*
> *(Ephesians 3:20–21, ESV, emphasis mine)*

In the last recorded prayer of Jesus, on the night before He was crucified, He prayed for His disciples:

> *"I will remain in the world no longer, but they are still in the world, and I am coming to you. Holy Father, protect them by the power of your name, the name you gave me, **so that they may be one as we are one**."*
>
> *(John 17:11, emphasis mine)*

And, He prayed for us—His Dwelling, His Body, His Bride:

> *"My prayer is not for them alone. I pray also for those who will believe in me through their message, **that all of them may be one**, Father, just as you are in me and I am in you. May they also be in us so that the world may believe that you have sent me. I have given them the glory that you gave me, **that they may be one as we are one**—I in them and you in me—so that they may be brought to complete unity. Then the world will know that you sent me and have loved them even as you have loved me."*
>
> *(John 17:20–23, emphasis mine)*

The Call to Unity

Paul exhorts us to let Jesus's desire for our unity become our attitude as well:

> *May the God who gives endurance and encouragement give you the same attitude of mind toward each other that Christ Jesus had, so that with one mind and one voice you may glorify the God and Father of our Lord Jesus Christ.*
>
> *(Romans 15:5–6)*

Paul continues in that same passage to give us some practical counsel: "Accept one another, then, just as Christ accepted you, in order to bring praise to God" (Romans 15:7). Accept one another. Welcome one another. Open your hearts to one another. Contend for one another.

I've written this book for women, but the call to oneness is not just about you and me. This is about *all* of us, men and women *together*. *Together* we are His body and His dwelling place. *Together* we are the bride of Christ. *Together* we bear the image of God.

The Enemy has amassed a great arsenal against our being built together in unity. We are prone to picking up weapons from his stockpile! Arrogance and dominance, self-pity and withdrawal, comparison and criticism, self-centeredness and self-absorption, unforgiveness and independence . . . these things stifle our own hearts as well as the hearts around us. They keep us from pursuing fellowship with other believers and move us toward isolation.

We must not allow these tools of the Enemy to have a place among us. Let's ask the Lord to help us identify these weapons when our hearts begin to take them up. As we ask Him to help us open our hearts and lives to each other, we *know* He will help because it's His will:

> *This is the confidence we have in approaching God: that if we ask anything according to his will, he hears us. And if we know that he hears us—whatever we ask—we know that we have what we asked of him.*
>
> *(1 John 5:14-15)*

Just as our individual hearts are in process, so this Dwelling, this Body, this Bride is in process. We come together in different states of maturity and seasons of life. Each of us, as we behold the glory of Jesus, is becoming more and more like Him. Paul refers to this as "being transformed into His image from one degree of glory to another" (see 2 Corinthians 3:18). More glory each day, each season, each year.

Sisters, our hearts are on a glory-to-glory journey together. This requires them to be teachable and flexible and vulnerable—all things I do *not* prefer. I would rather go through life knowing exactly what to do, how to do it, and when to do it. I want to cross tasks off my list and get on to the next thing—preferably one I am comfortable with and confident that I can do pretty well. Just show me my spot, and I'll do a good job of staying there. Put my stone in the third row above the foundation, fifth from the corner. I'll be a faithful stone in the temple wall, and I won't have to figure anything else out. That stone will represent a pretty dull heart. Not much glory there.

Let's join ourselves to Jesus's heart and let Him lead us in our relationships. God doesn't want us to do only what we're good at, or to forge a place for ourselves among people we are comfortable with. *Jesus* is building His Church! We are *being* built, not doing our own building. We do not have the blueprints. A whole heart understands it is on a journey and will not look for peace by "arriving." Our passions, thoughts, and purposes will find peace in relationship with Jesus and His people while we are on this journey with other hearts. Our hearts are becoming whole—together.

Chapter 19 Reflection

1. What does it mean to be "members of one another" (Romans 12:5)? How does that change how you think about relationships and fellowship?

_____

_____

_____

2. Consider the three pictures that we are given about our oneness: The Body of Christ, the temple of God's Spirit, the Bride of Christ. What does each of those pictures speak to you about how we relate to Jesus, to each other, and to those outside the Church?

_____

_____

_____

3. Jesus prayed that we would be one, just as the Godhead is one. In what ways do your actions and attitudes cooperate with that desire of Jesus? In what ways have you unintentionally sabotaged His desire?

_____

_____

_____

_____

Chapter 20

Thirsty Hearts

T he world has changed a lot since the fifties. I remember standing in the backyard with my dad watching Sputnik, the world's only satellite, moving across the sky. Space is now cluttered with thousands of satellites facilitating how we learn, how we play, how we communicate, what we watch, how my Safeway stays stocked, and how I pay for those groceries.

Yes, it's a changing world, but the human heart is still as precious and as vulnerable as it was in the fifties and all the way back in the Garden. Many of the dangers to the human heart are the same as they've always been. Many old afflictions have new disguises. I cannot conclude this book by promising a "safe" existence for your heart. I do not even hint at the possibility of keeping your heart cloistered from the storms of life that are always assaulting it.

The Bible does not give us hope that the world will become safer for our hearts. If anything, it's going to become *more* hazardous:

> *But mark this: There will be terrible times in the last days.*
> *People will be lovers of themselves, lovers of money, boastful,*

proud, abusive, disobedient to their parents, ungrateful, unholy, without love, unforgiving, slanderous, without self-control, brutal, not lovers of the good, treacherous, rash, conceited, lovers of pleasure rather than lovers of God.

(2 Timothy 3:1-4)

How can we pursue and maintain whole hearts while experiencing the things that wound them? It sounds like trying to recover from dehydration while you are still journeying through the desert. We might find an oasis and get temporary relief, but unless we can actually carry a water supply, we are stuck. The journey is too dangerous to continue, and we must stay where we are.

Ladies, here's the secret: we *can* carry water with us!

The Holy Spirit in You

All the water we need is available at all times. Every time our hearts feel dry and begin to shrivel up, we can take a drink that will revive them. Every time our hearts feel dirty and in need of cleansing, we have fresh water at our fingertips. Whenever our hearts feel cold and hard, there is calming water to soothe and soften.

The Bible describes followers of Jesus as those who have springs of living water flowing from within them:

> *On the last and greatest day of the festival, Jesus stood and said in a loud voice, "Let anyone who is thirsty come to me and drink. Whoever believes in me, as Scripture has said, rivers of living water will flow from within them." By this he meant the Spirit, whom those who believed in him were later to receive. Up to that time the Spirit had not been given, since Jesus had not yet been glorified.*

(John 7:37-39)

The rivers of living water Jesus spoke of are from the Holy Spirit, whom we talked about in Chapter 6. The Passion Translation puts it like this: "We can now experience the endless love of God cascading into our hearts through the Holy Spirit who lives in us" (Romans 5:5, TPT).

This love becomes a cascading river of living water that flows from *within* you. You don't have to get to the fountain to take a drink. The fountain is flowing inside you! The very presence of Jesus dwelling within you, through the Holy Spirit, is your heart's source of protection, restoration, and life.

Jesus said it like this to a Samaritan woman He encountered at a well, in John 4:

> *Everyone who drinks of this water will be thirsty again, but whoever drinks of the water that I will give him will never be thirsty again. The water that I will give him will become in him a spring of water welling up to eternal life.*
>
> *(John 4:13–14, ESV)*

Jesus is the source, and He is also our example. Jesus left the pleasures and privileges of heaven and became a man, living like us in this fallen world. He lived amid opposition and confusion. He was constantly pursued by forces that mocked, ridiculed, discredited, opposed, hated, abused, and ultimately killed him. He experienced the pain of loss and the sorrow of separation from God. But his heart remained free of the hopelessness and bitterness that assault our hearts. His body was torn, but His heart remained whole. Jesus put on flesh, but His heart remained in fellowship with heaven. He remained connected to the river of living water—the Holy Spirit—and He knew how to access it perfectly. His heart was drinking from heaven while His body was on the earth.

How We Stay Connected

Our hearts were made for heaven, and they must be nourished from there. David articulates the cry of a heart that cannot connect to those heavenly resources: "O God, you are my God; earnestly I seek you; my soul thirsts for you; my flesh faints for you, as in a dry and weary land where there is no water" (Psalm 63:1, ESV).

A woman who has not yet been restored to God does not have access to the resources of heaven. An unsaved heart is limited to the resources of this dry and weary land. But when we are born again, we actually become citizens of the kingdom of heaven: "Our citizenship is in heaven. And we eagerly await a Savior from there, the Lord Jesus Christ" (Philippians 3:20).

We confidently look forward to the day our King brings heaven to the earth. But until then, we are not limited to the unsavory and unhealthy sustenance of this fallen world. Our citizenship *is* in heaven. Present tense. Now. We are alive with Christ, with full access to His kingdom. Our hearts cannot heal, grow, or thrive outside that kingdom, but we are not outsiders! We have full rights to those heavenly resources, and we can learn how to access them. We *must* learn how to access them.

We can learn to steward our hearts as Jesus stewarded His own. Jesus kept His heart anchored in His Father's kingdom, so His heart's responses emanated from that reality. His *inner fountain of passion, thought, and purpose* had unhindered access to love, refreshment, nourishment, comfort, forgiveness, wisdom, self-control, peace—everything a heart needs to remain whole. We have that same access. We're just not good at staying there. We are not good at abiding like we are instructed to! The Apostle John reminded us in his gospel of Jesus's words, "Abide in me [Jesus], and I in you. As the branch cannot bear fruit by itself, unless it abides in the vine, neither can you, unless you abide in me" (John 15:4, ESV). He later wrote to the church, emphasizing this important truth: "And now, little children, abide in him" (1 John 2:28, ESV).

Jesus modeled two things our hearts can do to help us abide. First, He said to stay connected! Jesus likened it to being a branch that must stay connected to the vine. And how did He do it? He talked to His Father. He prayed! Luke described this in His Gospel: "Jesus often withdrew to lonely places and prayed" (Luke 5:16).

Jesus prayed long prayers: "One of those days Jesus went out to a mountainside to pray, and spent the night praying to God" (Luke 6:12). And He prayed short prayers. Jesus made it clear that length does not equal effectiveness when we pray. His model prayer, which we call the Lord's Prayer, is succinct:

> *"And when you pray, do not keep on babbling like pagans, for they think they will be heard because of their many words. Do not be like them, for your Father knows what you need before you ask him. This, then, is how you should pray: 'Our Father in heaven, hallowed be your name, your kingdom come, your will be done, on earth as it is in heaven. Give us today our daily bread. And forgive us our debts, as we also have forgiven our debtors. And lead us not into temptation, but deliver us from the evil one.'"*
>
> *(Matthew 6:7-13)*

Sometimes Jesus prayed alone, and sometimes He took some disciples with Him. Sometimes He snuck away at night when nothing else was happening. Other times He boldly walked away from his adoring crowds to be with the Father. People brought their kids to Him, and He prayed for those children. He prayed for His disciples. He prayed for you and me. He prayed while He was facing impending doom in the Garden of Gethsemane. And He prayed while He was on the cross.

Prayer is simply communicating with God, and you can do it any time, any place. Maintaining a dialogue with the Father is central to staying connected to that river of living water. "Help me, Jesus!" is a simple, fruitful prayer. "Thank you." "I need . . ." "I love You." "Forgive me." "Help me forgive." "Show me what to do." "I trust You." "Thank You for loving me."

Get creative about ways to find a minute to look into Jesus's eyes! I recently confided to a group of women that when I was a young mother, I would take an extra minute or two—or ten—in the bathroom, because some days, that was all the time I could take for myself. Almost all of them confessed to similar strategies. Do whatever it takes!

God already knows what you're going to ask, and He is quick to listen! Prayer is not about getting information to God; He already knows it all! Prayer is about taking your eyes off the world and connecting your heart to living water. Prayer turns your heart from the problem and focuses it on the One with solutions.

Do not entertain a definition of prayer that makes it out of reach for you. The Enemy would have us believe prayer is a formal activity that must be accompanied by quiet and solemnity. He would have us think we need space to prepare our hearts and minds before we approach God. But this is one place where our position is entirely different from Esther's! She had to prepare herself and enter formally, hoping the king would extend the golden scepter. But Jesus has already made a way for us. We get to barge into the throne room with our whole lives in disarray and blurt out our requests to a Father who invites us onto His lap and comforts us while He's listening. Paul assures us, "In him [Jesus] and through faith in him we may approach God with freedom and confidence" (Ephesians 3:12).

Do not downplay the importance and effectiveness of those quick prayers. But let one of those quick prayers be this: "Father, show me how to spend even more time with You!" A quick drink will revive a weary heart for a moment, but our hearts need time to rest: "He leads me beside still waters. He restores my soul" (Psalm 23:2–3, ESV).

Is your heart happy? Share it with Him. Angry? Confused? Fearful? Lonely? Take it to Him. My heart aches so much at times! Sometimes I can't even pray; all I can do is sob. I just sit on His lap and let it run its course. And then I let Him quiet me. I entrust my heart to Him. A sob is communication. It is my prayer. A quieting touch is His answer. My heart is drinking.

Prayer, like relationship, is a two-way thing. Let's not just share our hearts with Him; let's listen to His heart. Our hearts must feed on His truth, His wisdom, His perspective. He promises to speak to us, and He says we can learn to recognize His voice:

> *Whether you turn to the right or to the left, your ears will hear a voice behind you, saying, "This is the way; walk in it.*
>
> *(Isaiah 31:21)*

> *"My sheep hear my voice."*
>
> *(John 10:27, ESV)*

> *This is what the LORD says, he who made the earth, the LORD who formed it and established it—the LORD is his name: "Call to me and I will answer you and tell you great and unsearchable things you do not know."*
>
> *(Jeremiah 33:2-3)*

Can you imagine the "great and unsearchable things" that fill God's heart? Oh, how our hearts would love to drink of the deep mysteries of God's love!

Talking to God reminds our hearts their anchor is in another kingdom. The way is open so we can carry on a constant dialogue with Him. Jesus *knew* He was a citizen of another place, and His heart maintained fellowship in that other place. Let's follow His example.

The Walk of Obedience

The second thing Jesus modeled for us was obedience. He abided in His Father's will. It is impossible to stay close to God while intentionally turning our backs on His ways.

We have talked much about God's design for our lives. His ways are rooted in His love for us and His desire for our good. They are also rooted in His ultimate plan to fill the earth with His glory. His ways oppose everything that hinders the revelation of His goodness on the earth. For this reason, He does not offer His ways as mere suggestions to us. He calls them commandments. And we cannot abide in Him without submitting to his ways. Jesus told His disciples:

> *"As the Father has loved me, so have I loved you. Abide in my love. If you keep my commandments, you will abide in my love, just as I have kept my Father's commandments and abide in his love."*
>
> *(John 15:9-10, ESV)*

Does your heart balk at the word "commandment"? It certainly is a word that has had negative connotations. The commands of God have been misrepresented as things that must be done to earn salvation. "Blow it, and off to hell you go!" we fear Him saying. But that is *not* the heart of God.

The Enemy has taken the word "obedience" and made it look like a ball and chain. Let's reclaim the word and speak it to our hearts as a blessing from God Himself. *All God's ways are intended to nurture and protect your heart.* God is motivated by a desire to see your heart restored to His original design. His glory will be revealed in a planet full of whole hearts.

When my two boys were little, we lived in a house on a busy street. We had no backyard, and the front yard was small and unfenced. I longed to turn my kids loose outside so they could enjoy the sunshine (and I could enjoy a bit of quiet). But if they went outside, I had to go with them and watch them closely. They did not get to go outside as often as their hearts desired. One day, one of those little hearts found a way to sneak outside anyway. Before I knew he had escaped, someone knocked on our door, held him up, and said, "Is this your baby?" She had stopped her car because he was in the street.

Besides being an extreme embarrassment for me, this episode wrote a special truth on my heart. Fences are good things. My sons would *not* have liked a fence in that yard; they would have assumed it was there to keep them from having fun. But a fence actually would have permitted them to safely enjoy much more freedom.

A commandment is a fence for your heart. God is not glorified by making demands that rob mankind of joy and satisfaction! He is glorified as our hearts are fulfilled, loving Him, and loving each other. Love is at the center of His commandments:

> *For the commandments, "You shall not commit adultery, You shall not murder, You shall not steal, You shall not covet," and any other commandment, are summed up in this word: "You shall love your neighbor as yourself."*
>
> *(Romans 13:9, ESV)*

> *"This is my commandment, that you love one another as I have loved you."*
>
> *(John 15:12, ESV)*

Whole hearts are not dependent on perfect obedience—which is a good thing, because I cannot perfectly obey. I can take a stab at those commandments that target my actions. But God's command to love each other goes far deeper than actions. Not only am I to restrain myself from murdering someone, but I am to restrain what I think and say about them (see Matthew 5)! I have so far successfully refrained from murdering anyone, but I have definitely had angry thoughts. I have not loved well in all I say or think about others. I am certainly not always successful at loving my enemies or blessing someone who has just offended me.

The good news is God does not stand back to see if we will obey. His heart is zealously engaged in our pursuit of whole hearts. For the times we blow it in thought, word, or deed, He has purchased our forgiveness. As we ask for and receive His forgiveness, the blemishes on our hearts are erased. And as we reset our hearts toward obedience, He works from the inside to transform our passions, thoughts, and purposes:

> *"I will give you a new heart and put a new spirit in you; I will remove from you your heart of stone and give you a heart of flesh. And I will put my Spirit in you and move you to follow my decrees and be careful to keep my laws."*
>
> *(Ezekiel 36:26-27)*

God is making our hearts new! We can—and will!—abide in Him by following Jesus's example of obedience.

Jesus also gave us a picture of what it looks like to follow Him in obedience: "Take my yoke upon you and learn from me, for I am gentle and humble in heart, and you will find rest for your souls. For my yoke is easy and my burden is light" (Matthew 11:29-30).

Jesus's listeners would have clearly understood what Jesus was saying. They were a farming culture, and their plows were often pulled by pairs of oxen joined by a wooden frame called a yoke on their necks. The purpose of a yoke was to cause the animals to work together as one. Often a young ox was trained by being yoked with a stronger, more mature ox. The mature ox would do most of the work, and the younger one only needed to keep in step. If the younger one tried to follow its own path, the yoke would become burdensome and heavy.

Jesus's yoke is easy, but it *is* a yoke. His burden is light, but it *is* a burden. The path to a whole heart involves choosing to abide in Jesus by *taking up a yoke*. There is substance to this life; it is not a life of careless, self-serving choices. Those careless choices do not come with the promise of rest for our souls.

We are yoking ourselves to Someone who has preceded us in obedience. He understood His obedience would be costly, *and* it would bring joy to Him and to us! He knows obedience will be costly for us too, and we will lose heart if we do not take hold of the same attitude. The author of Hebrews encourages us:

> *We must let go of every wound that has pierced us and the sin we so easily fall into. Then we will be able to run life's marathon race with passion and determination, for the path has been already marked out before us. We look away from the natural realm and we fasten our gaze onto Jesus who birthed faith within us and who leads us forward into faith's perfection. His example is this: Because his heart was focused on the joy of knowing that you would be his, he endured the agony of the cross and conquered its humiliation, and now sits exalted at the right hand of the throne of God! So consider carefully how Jesus faced such intense opposition from sinners who opposed their own souls, so that you won't become worn down and cave in under life's pressures.*
> *(Hebrews 12:1-3, TPT)*

A whole heart does not need to shield itself from the hazards of this world. I do not need to fear a journey in the desert if I carry an unlimited supply of water. In fact, I can continue this journey expecting to bring a drink to a thirsty person along the way. This desert journey will not last forever! My destination is a glorious kingdom where all hearts are whole and there is no shortage of living water.

The Apostle John caught a glimpse of our eternal dwelling place with Jesus, where nothing will inhibit our access:

> *Then the angel showed me the river of the water of life, bright*
> *as crystal, flowing from the throne of God and of the Lamb*
> *through the middle of the street of the city.*
> *(Revelation 22:1-2, ESV)*

Dear friends, the time is coming when we will never thirst again. Until then, let's practice allowing our hearts to abide in the Source of living, healing water.

Chapter 20 Reflection

1. What does it mean to live in this world but keep your heart anchored in Jesus's Kingdom? What would it look like for you personally? What habits and practices are working for you now? Ask the Lord to lead you into new ways of staying connected and drinking!

_____

_____

_____

_____

_____

_____

2. Have you experienced troubles that have actually led you deeper into God's love and provision?

_____

_____

_____

_____

_____

_____

_____

_____

3. Are you weary and thirsty now? Are you currently in the middle of a trial that you would like to use as an opportunity to experience more of Him?

_____

_____

_____

_____

_____

_____

4. Does it seem possible for you to be someone who can bring a drink to others who are weary and thirsty? How would your passions, thoughts, and purposes have to be transformed?

_____

_____

_____

_____

_____

_____

_____

_____

Chapter 21

Waiting Hearts

I love growing old. I mean that. A younger body has its appeal, but I would never trade in this old heart for physical youth. My heart has aged through a journey of incredible joys, gut-wrenching sorrows, and a whole spectrum of delights and challenges in between. And through it all, God has been with me. Through the waters and through the fire, He has been faithful to comfort and transform me.

There were times when all I could do was hang on to what felt like a far-off promise, clinging to God through the dark mystery. Many things are still mysteries to me. But with the benefit of time, I can look back and see Jesus has never let go of me, and He has never wavered in His commitment to my complete restoration. Over and over, I have experienced God's power and grace in using hardships to heal and deepen my heart rather than allowing them to damage it.

There are circumstances in my life I still can't see any blessed resolution to, but my heart knows His presence and comfort, and I can leave those things in His hands. I can say with Paul: "I know whom I have believed, and am convinced that he is able to guard what I have entrusted to him until that day" (2 Timothy 1:12).

I have a lot of living left to do. My husband and I are technically retired, but may I never retire from pursuing a whole heart! I have not yet grasped all that Jesus bought for me. And I will not grasp it all in this body. But whether my remaining time on Earth is long or short, whether I am in good or ill health, my heart will keep growing. There will always be more treasure:

> *Brothers and sisters, I do not consider myself yet to have taken hold of it. But one thing I do: Forgetting what is behind and straining toward what is ahead, I press on toward the goal to win the prize for which God has called me heavenward in Christ Jesus.*
>
> *(Philippians 3:13-14)*

A popular bumper sticker from the eighties proclaimed, "Life's a b****h and then you die." The phrase is still popular, popping up in songs, coffee cups, and T-shirts. It is a statement that graphically and tragically describes the life of the brokenhearted, a life that starts off hurting with no hope of improvement. For as long as they reside on the earth, they expect their hearts to remain pained, unfulfilled, and assaulted. The horror and emptiness will continue until they fade away into the abyss of death. This is the hopelessness that was released on the earth in the garden. This is an existence without God.

We whose hearts have come alive to God have a new bumper sticker: "Surely goodness and love will follow me all the days of my life, and I will dwell in the house of the LORD forever" (Psalm 23:6).

This is what a whole heart feels like! For starters, we *expect* to encounter goodness and love. But this promise is severely understated in most translations. That Hebrew word for "follow" signifies an aggressive pursuit, not a passive following along behind. Goodness and love—in the form of God Himself—will *aggressively pursue* me all the days of my life. Check out these other situations where this same Hebrew verb is used:

> *When Abram heard that his relative had been taken captive, he called out the 318 trained men born in his household and went* **in pursuit** *as far as Dan. During the night Abram divided his men to attack them and he routed them,* **pursuing** *them as far as Hobah, north of Damascus.*
> *(Genesis 14:14–15, emphasis mine)*

> *You will* **pursue** *your enemies, and they will fall by the sword before you. Five of you will* **chase** *a hundred, and a hundred of you will* **chase** *ten thousand, and your enemies will fall by the sword before you.*
> *(Leviticus 26:7-8, emphasis mine)*

Goodness and love are *chasing* me! They are intent on catching me. And when my time comes, this happy pursuit comes to a glorious end! I won't just fade away. I will be received into the very presence of the goodness and love that have been pursuing me, and I will live in God's presence *forever.* My heart will no longer encounter the temptations and molestations of this world.

The Glorious End of the Story

You and I, together with all who are called by Christ's name, are waiting. Rich or poor, healthy or frail, overworked or bored, full of hope or full of doubt, alone or in a crowd . . . we are waiting. Waiting for that second coming of Jesus when everything will be made new and our hearts will be free of this fallen world. That is the glorious end of our story . . . but really, it's not an end at all. It will be the culmination of all things temporal, and the beginning of a glorious eternity with Him. Until then, we wait. Some of us will be waiting until the end of our lives on Earth. Some who are reading this book may very well be alive when Jesus returns. Either way, we wait.

But let's not let our hearts get lulled into passive waiting! Our hearts can remain vulnerable to the One who created them and is restoring them. We can be teachable and hopeful like King David: "Search me, God, and know my heart; test me and know my anxious thoughts. See if there is any offensive way in me, and lead me in the way everlasting" (Psalm 139:23-24).

We live in in-between times. Jesus's work is complete; from the cross He proclaimed, "It is finished." Satan has been defeated, but he has been allowed to have influence until Jesus's kingdom comes in its fullness. We are already citizens of heaven, but our feet are still bound to a fallen earth. Freedom has already been purchased, but we still experience bondage. Jesus purchased whole hearts for us, but our hearts are still in process.

If our waiting hearts are anchored in eternity, we will find strength and joy as we keep our eyes on Jesus. He looked forward to the joy of having our hearts restored to Him. We look forward to experiencing the fullness of that restoration:

> . . . *fixing our eyes on Jesus, the pioneer and perfecter of faith. For the joy set before him he endured the cross, scorning its shame, and sat down at the right hand of the throne of God. Consider him who endured such opposition from sinners, so that you will not grow weary and lose heart.*
>
> *(Hebrews 12:2-3)*

We won't always get it right. Instead of forgiving and receiving comfort, we may let injustices penetrate beyond the power and presence of love. We may invite the forces of comparison or retaliation to formulate plans in our hearts. We may let arrogance and bitterness rise within us. Our hearts may become vindictive and hard. Walls may go up. We may lose our peace and joy. The rest of the world may not always see the glory of God in us.

But let's not give up! These temporary setbacks do not define us! Let's live with our eyes fixed on God's promises, not on our weaknesses. God's promises for our hearts are true, and by His grace we can keep moving forward: "Since, then, you have been raised with Christ, set your hearts on things above, where Christ is, seated at the right hand of God" (Colossians 3:1). Paul also reminds us to stay encouraged:

> *Therefore we do not lose heart. Though outwardly we are wasting away, yet inwardly we are being renewed day by day. For our light and momentary troubles are achieving for us an eternal glory that far outweighs them all. So we fix our eyes not on what is seen, but on what is unseen, since what is seen is temporary, but what is unseen is eternal.*
>
> *(2 Corinthians 4:16-18)*

I believe the Lord is calling us to engage proactively in the stewardship of our hearts like never before. We may have blessed times where things seem so good, we feel we can disregard diligence in the care of our hearts. We may have times so difficult, we want to ignore our hearts and let them shut down altogether. Dear sister, whatever life looks like for you now, do not give in to the temptation to neglect or shut down your heart.

I am not suggesting your heart cannot rest. In fact, it *must* rest. But true rest is diligent and purposeful. It is not a matter of doing nothing, but of actively abiding in Jesus. Rest requires a heart that keeps pursuing Jesus. Here are some promises about resting:

> *"Come to me, all you who are weary and burdened, and I will give you rest."*
>
> *(Matthew 11:28)*

God is the strength of my heart and my portion forever.

(Psalm 73:26)

Let's take Jesus's hand and open our hearts to his transforming love!
Let's treasure our hearts like He does and care for them well. We are safe
on this journey as we:

Abide in Jesus, as branches cling to a vine.

Stay yoked to Jesus, as ones who are learning and maturing.

Keep communicating, as ones who are in love.

Keep asking, as ones who are dependent.

Keep trusting, as the daughters of a perfect Father.

Keep obeying, as ones who expect joy.

And stay hopeful, as ones who are being pursued by a Lover who will
not give up the chase.

Jesus revealed the end of mankind's journey to the Apostle John, and
it has been recorded for our hearts to take hold of:

> *Then I saw a new heaven and a new earth, for the first heaven
> and the first earth had passed away, and there was no longer
> any sea. I saw the Holy City, the new Jerusalem, coming down
> out of heaven from God, prepared as a bride beautifully dressed
> for her husband. And I heard a loud voice from the throne
> saying, 'Look! God's dwelling place is now among the people,
> and he will dwell with them. They will be his people, and God
> himself will be with them and be their God. He will wipe every
> tear from their eyes. There will be no more death or mourning
> or crying or pain, for the old order of things has passed away.*
>
> *He who was seated on the throne said, "I am making everything
> new!" Then he said, "Write this down, for these words are
> trustworthy and true." He said to me: "It is done. I am the*

Alpha and the Omega, the Beginning and the End. To the thirsty I will give water without cost from the spring of the water of life. Those who are victorious will inherit all this, and I will be their God and they will be my children."

(Revelation 21:1-7)

John speaks for all of us: "The Spirit and the bride say, 'Come!' And let the one who hears say, 'Come!' Let the one who is thirsty come; and let the one who wishes take the free gift of the water of life" (Revelation 22:17). Let's join our hearts together and "come." The end of this journey will be glorious. All things will be new. Our hearts will be whole, forever. Until then, dear sisters, let's take Jesus's hand, care for our hearts, and take this glory-to-glory journey together!

Chapter 21 Reflection

1. Do you have a hard time reconciling God's goodness with the miseries you see around you? Is your heart able to find peace while we wait for the restoration of all things?

_____

_____

_____

_____

_____

_____

2. Have you experienced God's comfort at times during the journey through this book?

_____

_____

_____

_____

_____

_____

_____

3. This chapter suggests two opposing outlooks on life:

   "Life's a b****h, and then you die," and

   "Surely goodness and love will follow me all the days of my life, and I will dwell in the house of the Lord forever."

   What has your heart's journey felt like in the past? Have you experienced the desperation of the first quote? Are you beginning to grasp the truth and joy of the second quote? Take time to talk to Jesus about how your heart is feeling, and let Him speak to you as you continue this journey!

_____

_____

_____

_____

_____

_____

_____

_____

_____

_____

_____

_____

_____

_____

About the Author

L aura Knutson has over forty years' experience in women's ministry, Bible study, worship, and prayer. Her ministry to women has included teaching, mentoring, personal counseling, leading retreats, and heading up women's ministries in her local church.

Laura enjoys time with family, road trips, and classical music. She has been married to her husband, Mark, for forty-five years. They have two grown sons and five grandchildren, and make their home in Puyallup, Washington.

You can visit Laura's website at:
www.thewholeheartedwoman.me

A free ebook edition is available with the purchase of this book.

To claim your free ebook edition:

1. Visit MorganJamesBOGO.com
2. Sign your name CLEARLY in the space
3. Complete the form and submit a photo of the entire copyright page
4. You or your friend can download the ebook to your preferred device

Morgan James BOGO™

A **FREE** ebook edition is available for you or a friend with the purchase of this print book.

CLEARLY SIGN YOUR NAME ABOVE

Instructions to claim your free ebook edition:
1. Visit MorganJamesBOGO.com
2. Sign your name CLEARLY in the space above
3. Complete the form and submit a photo of this entire page
4. You or your friend can download the ebook to your preferred device

Print & Digital Together Forever.

Snap a photo

Free ebook

Read anywhere